• Up-to-Date
• Easy to Use
• All Tests
• No Fillers

ISBN 0-8373-6403-5
3 REGENTS COMPETENCY TEST SERIES

RUDMAN'S QUESTIONS AND ANSWERS ON THE...

RCT

Regents Competency Test in...

Reading

Test Preparation Study Guide
Questions & Answers

NLC
NATIONAL LEARNING CORPORATION

PLASTIC BOUND—LIES FLAT FOR STUDY EASE!

ISBN 0-8373-6403-5

3 Regents Competency Test Series

Regents Competency Test in...

Reading

Test Preparation Study Guide

Questions & Answers

NATIONAL LEARNING CORPORATION

National Learning Corporation

212 Michael Drive, Syosset, New York 11791

(516) 921-8888
(800) 645-6337
FAX: (516) 921-8743
www.passbooks.com
sales @ passbooks.com
info @ passbooks.com

PRINTED IN THE UNITED STATES OF AMERICA

PASSBOOK®

NOTICE

This book is SOLELY intended for, is sold ONLY to, and its use is RESTRICTED to *individual*, bona fide applicants or candidates who qualify by virtue of having seriously filed applications for appropriate license, certificate, professional and/or promotional advancement, higher school matriculation, scholarship, or other legitimate requirements of educational and/or governmental authorities.

This book is NOT intended for use, class instruction, tutoring, training, duplication, copying, reprinting, excerption, or adaptation, etc., by:

(1) Other publishers

(2) Proprietors and/or Instructors of "Coaching" and/or Preparatory Courses

(3) Personnel and/or Training Divisions of commercial, industrial, and governmental organizations

(4) Schools, colleges, or universities and/or their departments and staffs, including teachers and other personnel

(5) Testing Agencies or Bureaus

(6) Study groups which seek by the purchase of a single volume to copy and/or duplicate and/or adapt this material for use by the group as a whole without having purchased individual volumes for each of the members of the group

(7) Et al.

Such persons would be in violation of appropriate Federal and State statutes.

PROVISION OF LICENSING AGREEMENTS. — Recognized educational commercial, industrial, and governmental institutions and organizations, and others legitimately engaged in educational pursuits, including training, testing, and measurement activities, may address a request for a licensing agreement to the copyright owners, who will determine whether, and under what conditions, including fees and charges, the materials in this book may be used by them. In other words, a licensing facility exists for the legitimate use of the material in this book on other than an individual basis. However, it is asseverated and affirmed here that the material in this book *CANNOT* be used without the receipt of the express permission of such a licensing agreement from the Publishers.

NATIONAL LEARNING CORPORATION
212 Michael Drive
Syosset, New York 11791

Inquiries re licensing agreements should be addressed to:
The President
National Learning Corporation
212 Michael Drive
Syosset, New York 11791

PASSBOOK SERIES®

THE *PASSBOOK SERIES®* has been created to prepare applicants and candidates for the ultimate academic battlefield – the examination room.

At some time in our lives, each and every one of us may be required to take an examination – for validation, matriculation, admission, qualification, registration, certification, or licensure.

Based on the assumption that every applicant or candidate has met the basic formal educational standards, has taken the required number of courses, and read the necessary texts, the *PASSBOOK SERIES®* furnishes the one special preparation which may assure passing with confidence, instead of failing with insecurity. Examination questions – together with answers – are furnished as the basic vehicle for study so that the mysteries of the examination and its compounding difficulties may be eliminated or diminished by a sure method.

This book is meant to help you pass your examination provided that you qualify and are serious in your objective.

The entire field is reviewed through the huge store of content information which is succinctly presented through a provocative and challenging approach – the question-and-answer method.

A climate of success is established by furnishing the correct answers at the end of each test.

You soon learn to recognize types of questions, forms of questions, and patterns of questioning. You may even begin to anticipate expected outcomes.

You perceive that many questions are repeated or adapted so that you can gain acute insights, which may enable you to score many sure points.

You learn how to confront new questions, or types of questions, and to attack them confidently and work out the correct answers.

You note objectives and emphases, and recognize pitfalls and dangers, so that you may make positive educational adjustments.

Moreover, you are kept fully informed in relation to new concepts, methods, practices, and directions in the field.

You discover that you are actually taking the examination all the time: you are preparing for the examination by "taking" an examination, not by reading extraneous and/or supererogatory textbooks.

In short, this PASSBOOK®, used directedly, should be an important factor in helping you to pass your test.

NEW YORK STATE TESTING PROGRAM

New York has the oldest and the largest State testing program in the Nation. It began with the development and administration of the *preliminary* or eighth-grade Regents examinations in 1865, which provided a measure of accountability in the distribution of State funds to the various academies. Since that time, the testing program has been expanded and modified on numerous occasions to meet the changing needs of the schools, the Regents, and the State Education Department.

Presently, there are seven components of the State testing program. (See attached chart.) Each was created for a specific purpose in order to meet specific needs, and the test scores are used in a wide variety of ways. In general, however, the testing program developed and administered by the State serves the following purposes:

1. To Maintain Standards. The Board of Regents, the Commissioner of Education, and the State Education Department have as one of their primary functions ensuring that common educational standards are met in all school buildings in the State. The State testing program which involves all students in the State yields information about the extent to which State-set standards are being met.

2. To Influence Instruction. Since State tests, which are achievement tests based on Department-recommended courses of study, are used to evaluate the quality of instruction and learning that have taken place, they are a very strong influence on the breadth and depth of course content and on instructional practices.

3. To Provide Accountability. Public elementary and secondary education in the State consumes billions of dollars worth of resources each year. These resources come from revenue raised from taxes paid by State residents at the State and local level. Citizens of the State have a right to expect that public officials responsible for those expenditures are accountable for their effective use. In addition, parents and others, such as college admissions officers and future employers, have a right to know what is being achieved in State classrooms.

This accountability is generally accomplished by the State requirement that a comprehensive assessment report be presented to the public annually. At the local level, the comprehensive assessment report contains information about performance of students in each building and for the district as a whole. At the State level, reports such as the ANNUAL REPORT ON THE STATE OF EDUCATION to the Governor contain similar information for the State as a whole. State-developed and administered tests are an important component of the reports at both levels.

4. To Issue Credentials. The Board of Regents and the Commissioner of Education set requirements for graduation. Students demonstrate that they have met these requirements by passing State tests and by completing specified courses. The use of State tests ensures that a diploma in New York State has meaning in terms of levels of achievement no matter what school building in the State a student attends.

In addition, students may earn a Regents diploma by passing State examinations based on Regents-level courses of study. These courses of study are most often taken by college-bound students.

5. To Identify Students in Need of Remediation. Not all students in the State achieve at the same rate. Some students take longer than others to attain various achievement levels. One very important policy of the Board of Regents is that students who are falling behind in their achievement must be identified as soon as possible so that their deficit does not accumulate over time to the point that by the time they reach high school; they may not be able to meet the requirements set for graduation. Consequently, State tests are used to identify students who need instructional intervention in the early elementary grades and throughout their academic careers.

6. To Identify Buildings in Need of Assistance. Some buildings have large numbers of students who are not making adequate progress. It is also the policy of the Board of Regents to identify these buildings so that special attention and resources can be directed toward them. State-developed tests are a critical factor in the identification of these buildings.

7. To Distribute State Aid. State tests are also used to drive additional State aid to those students who need additional assistance. Federal Chapter 1 monies and State PSEN and PCEN funds are examples of programs whose purpose is to drive resources to students most in need. State tests are an important factor in the decision-making which determines which districts and students need additional resources.

8. To Provide Information for Local Decision-making. Selected State tests provide data that can be used for decision-making at the local level. Teachers use student test scores to assign final course grades; guidance counselors use student test scores to help students make college application decisions; and school administrators use test results to manage and evaluate their educational programs.

NEWYORK STATE TESTING PROGRAM COMPONENTS AND GRADES AT WHICH TESTS ARE ADMINISTERED

Component	Grade administered									
	3	4	5	6	7	8	9	10	11	12
Pupil Evaluation Program*										
Readings	x			x						
Mathematics	x			x						
Writing			x							
Program Evaluation Test*										
Science		x								
Social Studies				x		x				
Preliminary Competency Test**										
Readings						x	x			
Writing						x	x			
Regents Competency Tests**										
Readings									x	
Writing									x	
Mathematics							x			
Science							x			
Social Studies								x	x	
Regents Examinations**							x	x	x	x
Second Language Proficiency Examinations**						x				
Occupational Education Proficiency Examinations**							x	x	x	x

* All students tested at grade indicated
** Selected students tested

Unlike the education departments in most of the other states, the New York State Education Department develops its own tests, with the exception of the reading tests which use the Degrees of Reading Power (DRP) methodology. The development of State tests is a cooperative venture that involves hundreds of classroom teachers. Committees of teachers work on the planning of tests, the writing and revision of test questions, and the assembly and review of entire tests. The teachers bring to these tasks not only their own subject matter expertise, but also their knowledge of students' strengths and weaknesses. Their contribution to the State testing program is invaluable.

There are seven components of the State testing program, as described in the sections that follow. Each was created for a specific purpose in order to meet specific needs, and the test scores are used in a wide variety of ways. Yet, all State tests share three qualities: (1) they are all based on State-recommended or prescribed courses of study; (2) they are all intended to establish and maintain achievement standards; and (3) they all provide a measure of accountability for the State's elementary and secondary schools. Test results for each State test appear on the annual Comprehensive Assessment Reports for schools and school districts, providing a public record of school effectiveness and stimulating public dialogue leading to school improvement.

Regents Examinations

The program of high school Regents examinations began in 1878 to help the State's colleges make admissions decisions. Currently, 16 Regents examinations are offered in the areas of English, social studies, mathematics, sciences, and foreign languages. The examinations are intended for the college-bound and are taken by about 60 percent of the high school population. Examinations are administered under secure conditions on specified dates in January, June, and August. The answer papers are scored locally, and a sample of papers is called to the Education Department for review.

Most of the Regents examinations have a mix of essay or open ended questions and multiple choice questions. Only the science examinations consist either largely or entirely of multiple-choice questions. Scoring keys and scoring guides are provided to assure comparability in grading standards from school to school.

Regent's examination scores are used in a number of ways. They are used by teachers in the process of assigning course grades. They are used to demonstrate competency in those subjects in which competency is required for receipt of a local high school diploma, which is generally a more prestigious credential than a local high school diploma. They are used by guidance counselors in helping students make college-going decisions. And they are used by college admissions personnel to control for between-school differences in grading standards and practice

Pupil Evaluation Program Tests

The Pupil Evaluation Program (PEP) was initiated as a result of the federal Elementary and Secondary Education Act of 1965, which, under Title I, provided massive amounts of aid for teaching the basic skills to disadvantaged children. Currently, the program consists of reading and mathematics tests, which are administered in grades three and six, and a writing test administered in grade five. The tests are administered at prescribed times each spring. They are scored locally, and a sample of papers is reviewed in the Education Department.

While the writing and mathematics tests are developed in-house, the reading tests are obtained commercially. The reading tests use the Degrees of Reading Power (DRP) methodology, which provides reliable estimates of the level of reading material that a pupil can read with various degrees of success. The DRP system allows teachers to provide pupils with reading materials that are at the proper level of difficulty, or readability. The writing test requires the pupil to produce two writing samples, which are rated holistically. The mathematics tests are traditional mathematics tests based on the Department's K-6 mathematics syllabus.

PEP test scores, since 1979, have been used to identify pupils who are not making normal progress in developing the foundation skills of reading, writing, and mathematics. Pupils who score below the State Reference Point must be given appropriate remediation. The scores are also used in determining the amount of State aid that each district receives for Pupils with Special Education Needs (PSEU). Because every pupil is required to take the PEP tests, the scores obtained on the reading and the mathematics tests are widely used as indicators of school effectiveness.

Regents Competency Tests

Regents competency tests were first administered in 1979 and 1980. They were designed to establish minimum standards in reading, writing, and mathematics for receipt of a local high school diploma. The tests replaced an earlier set of competency tests that were widely perceived as setting too low a graduation standard. The new standards became effective for pupils graduating from high school in June 1981 and thereafter. As a general rule, the Regents competency tests are taken only by pupils who do not take Regents examinations and are not planning to attend college.

The Regents Action Plan, which was adopted in 1984, specified three additional areas in which pupils must demonstrate competency to receive a local high school diploma: science, global studies, and United States history and government. The science test measures key concepts and understandings developed in grades 7, 8, and 9. This test was administered for the· first time in June 1988, and competency in science was administered for the first time in 1991 The global studies test is based on the global studies course taught in grades 9 and 10. It was administered for the first time in June 1989, and competency in global studies has been required for graduation since 1992. The United States history and government test is based on the United States history course taught in grade 11. It was administered for the first time in June 1988, and competency in United States history and government became a requirement for graduation in 1990.

The Regents competency test in reading uses the Degrees of Reading Power methodology, through which the graduation standard in reading is directly linked to the average readability level of textbooks used in required high school courses. The writing test requires the pupil to produce three writing samples: a business letter, a report, and a composition. Pupil responses to the writing test prompts are rated holistically in the local school, and all papers scored 60 percent or higher (65 percent is passing) are sent to the Education Department for review. The Regents competency tests in mathematics consists of open-ended and multiple-choice questions sampling from objectives specified in the syllabus, General High School Mathematics. The Regents competency test in science is almost entirely objective, while the two Regents competency tests in social studies consist of both objective and essay sections.

With few exceptions, scores obtained on the Regents competency tests are used exclusively for the purpose of determining if pupils have attained diploma standards in the areas of reading, writing, mathematics, science, and social studies.

Preliminary Competency Tests

An important part of the Regents' competency testing program is the concept of early screening and intervention. As noted previously, pupils scoring below the State Reference Points on the Pupil Evaluation Program tests in reading, writing, or mathematics must be given appropriate remediation. The preliminary competency tests were created in 1979 to provide additional screening points in reading and writing in grades 8 or 9. Thus, in reading, pupils are screened in grades 3, 6, and 8 or 9 to determine if they are making satisfactory progress in the development of reading comprehension. In writing, pupils are screened in grades 5 and 8 or 9.

In both reading and writing, the preliminary competency tests are similar in scope and format to the Regents competency tests. The tests differ only in terms of level of difficulty. In general, preliminary competency test scores are used solely to identify pupils in need of remediation.

Program Evaluation Tests

The Regents Action Plan called for the creation of three new categories of tests. One was a group of three program evaluation tests: in elementary school science, in elementary school social studies, and in middle school social studies. The elementary school social studies test was administered for the first time in May 1987; the other two program evaluation tests were introduced in May 1989

The elementary school social studies test consists of two required parts that are administered at the end of grade 6 and an optional class participation project that can be administered at any time in grade 6. The two required parts are a series of objective questions and a writing exercise based on the K-6 social studies syllabus. The middle school test is given at the end of grade 8 and is based on the social studies syllabus for grades 7-8. This test is similar in format to the grade 6 social studies test. The elementary school science test is administered at the end of grade 4, measuring objectives taught in grades K-4. The test has a component consisting of objective questions and a manipulative skills component, both of which are required. Attitude measures are provided for optional use.

Unlike the PEP tests, the program evaluation tests are used exclusively to evaluate the effectiveness of instructional programs. Scores are not used to identify pupils in need of remediation and, for this reason, no State Reference Points have been established.

Second Language Proficiency Examinations

A secondary category of tests added by the Regents Action Plan is that of the second language proficiency examinations. These tests permit pupils to earn high school credit for the study of a second language in elementary and middle schools. These tests were administered for the first time in June 1989 in five of the languages in which Regents examinations are offered: French, German, Italian, Latin, and Spanish.

The second language proficiency examinations measure reading, writing, speaking, and listening skills, with an emphasis on the speaking and listening components. Pupils who pass a second language proficiency examination may earn the first unit of high school credit for foreign language study.

Occupational Education Proficiency Examinations

The third category of tests added by the Regents Action Plan is that of the occupational education proficiency examinations. These examinations help establish and maintain achievement standards in occupational education similar to those that exist in general education. The examinations are administered twice or three times each year under secure conditions.

The first of the occupational education proficiency examinations were administered during the 1987-88 school year. During that year, examinations were offered in the course Introduction to Occupations and in the areas of technology and home economics. Examinations in all other areas of concentration were added over the next several years. These examinations are paper-and-pencil tests, but performance testing components will be introduced subsequently.

Pupils must pass occupational education proficiency examinations in their areas of specialization to receive either a local or a Regents diploma.

REGENTS COMPETENCY TESTS

Regents competency tests were first administered in 1979 and 1980. They were designed to establish minimum standards in reading, writing, and mathematics for receipt of a local high school diploma. The tests replaced an earlier set of competency tests that were widely perceived as setting too Iowa graduation standard. The new standards became effective for pupils graduating from high school in June 1981 and thereafter. As a general rule, the Regents competency tests are taken only by pupils who do not take Regents examinations and are not planning to attend college.

In order to receive a high school diploma, students must demonstrate the ability to read and write. They may demonstrate this ability by passing either the Regents competency tests in reading and writing or the Regents comprehensive examination in English.

The Regents competency test in reading uses the Degrees of Reading Power CORP) methodology, through which the graduation standard in reading is directly linked to the average readability level of text books used in required high school courses. Thus, students passing the Regents competency test in reading have demonstrated the ability to read the textbooks used in New York State high schools to deliver the curriculum in the courses required for a local high school diploma.

The Regents competency test in reading is designed to measure students' ability to understand written materials of varying levels of difficulty. The tests consist of a series of nonfiction prose passages on a variety of topics. Each passage contains about 300 words. The passages are presented in order of difficulty, beginning- with easy material and progressing to difficult material. Seven words are omitted in each passage, and the most appropriate word must be selected from the five alternatives provided for each deleted word.

The test items are designed so that the text of the passages must be read and understood in order for the student to respond correctly. All of the response options *fit* the blank space; each one makes a grammatically correct and logically plausible sentence if the sentence is considered in isolation. However, only one response *fits* or is plausible when the surrounding context of the passage is considered. Thus, the selection of the correct response depends on understanding the prose in the surrounding text. Students should be able to respond correctly to all or nearly all items in the text to the point where they cannot understand a passage sufficiently well to decide which word is the correct choice.

The deleted words and the other response options are words in common use and are of uniform difficulty throughout the test. Thus, the test items become more difficult only with respect to the difficulty of the text in the passages. All of the information that is needed to select the correct response is provided in the text of the passages; there is no need to supply information from memory or past experience. Only the ability to process sentences for meaning is required for success on the test.

The Regents competency test in writing is a direct measure of students' ability to organize and present ideas in written form. The test consists of three different types of writing tasks: a business letter, a report, and a composition. In the business letter, the students request corrective action because of a problem such as failure to receive a product ordered by mail, defective processing of film, or unsatisfactory repair of an item. In the report, students reorganize a set of notes and write a unified report for a specific audience. Subjects include a meeting on energy resources, an interview with a performer, and a visit to a local industry. The composition requires writing that is based on one of four purposes for writing: description, narration, explanation, or persuasion.

Students' responses to the writing test prompts are rated holistically in the local school, and all papers rated 60 percent or higher (65 percent is passing) are sent to the State Education Department for review and confirmation of the school's pass/fail decision.

With few exceptions, the scores obtained on these Regents competency tests are used exclusively for the purpose of determining if students have attained diploma standards in the areas of reading and writing.

The Regents comprehensive examination in English tests students' listening skills, knowledge of vocabulary, spelling ability, level of reading comprehension, and writing ability. The listening skills section requires students to listen to a selection for purposes such as discovering the speaker's purpose, acquiring information, and evaluating the speaker's message. The reading comprehension section typically consists of three passages representative of various literary genre; e.g., poetry, nonfiction, and fiction. The questions based on the passages require students to examine the author's use of language and literary devices, to determine general text characteristics, and to draw inferences based upon the content of the passage. Students' writing ability is tested by requiring them to write an essay based on works of literature and a composition based on a given situation or a given topic.

The Regents Action Plan, which was adopted in 1984, specified three additional areas in which pupils must demonstrate competency to receive a local high school diploma: science, global studies, and United States history and government. The science test measures key concepts and understandings developed in grades 7, 8, and 9. This test was administered for the first time in June 1988, and competency in science has been required for graduation beginning in 1991. The global studies test is based on the global studies course taught in grades 9 and 10. An experimental edition of the test was administered for the first time in June 1989, and competency in global studies has been required for graduation beginning in 1992. The United States history and government test is based on the United States history course taught in grade 11. An experimental edition of the test was administered for the first time in June 1988, and competency in United States history and government became a requirement for graduation in 1990.

The Regents competency test in reading uses the Degrees of Reading Power methodology, through which the graduation standard in reading is directly linked to the average readability level of textbooks used in required high school courses. The writing test requires the pupil to produce three writing samples: a business letter, a report, and a composition. Pupil responses to the writing test prompts are rated holistically in the local school, and all papers scored 60 percent or higher (65 percent in passing) are sent to the Education Department for review. The Regents competency test in mathematics consists of open-ended and multiple-choice questions sampling from objectives specified in the syllabus, General High School Mathematics. The Regents competency test in science is almost entirely objective, while the two Regents competency tests in social studies consist of both objective and essay sections.

The regents competency tests, the grades at which they are administered, and the purpose of the tests are shown below.

Test	Grade Administered	Purpose of the Tests
RCT-Mathematics	9	To assure that all pupils receiving a high-school diploma have achieved a minimum standard of proficiency in the basic skills of reading, writing, mathematics, science and social studies.
RCT-Science	9	
RCT-Reading	11/12	
RCT-Writing	11/12	To establish minimum standards for a high-school diploma.
RCT-Global Studies	10	
RCT-United States History and Government	11	

HOW TO TAKE A TEST

You have studied long, hard and conscientiously.

With your official admission card in hand, and your heart pounding, you have been admitted to the examination room.

You note that there are several hundred other applicants in the examination room waiting to take the same test.

They all appear to be equally well prepared.

You know that nothing but your best effort will suffice. The "moment of truth" is at hand: you now have to demonstrate objectively, in writing, your knowledge of content and your understanding of subject matter.

You are fighting the most important battle of your life—to pass and/or score high on an examination which will determine your career and provide the economic basis for your livelihood.

What extra, special things should you know and should you do in taking the examination?

BEFORE THE TEST

YOUR PHYSICAL CONDITION IS IMPORTANT

If you are not well, you can't do your best work on tests. If you are half asleep, you can't do your best either. Here are some tips:

1) Get about the same amount of sleep you usually get. Don't stay up all night before the test, either partying or worrying—DON'T DO IT!
2) If you wear glasses, be sure to wear them when you go to take the test. This goes for hearing aids, too.
3) If you have any physical problems that may keep you from doing your best, be sure to tell the person giving the test. If you are sick or in poor health, you really cannot do your best on any test. You can always come back and take the test some other time.

AT THE TEST

EXAMINATION TECHNIQUES

1) Read the general instructions carefully. These are usually printed on the first page of the exam booklet. As a rule, these instructions refer to the timing of the examination; the fact that you should not start work until the signal and must stop work at a signal, etc. If there are any *special* instructions, such as a choice of questions to be answered, make sure that you note this instruction carefully.

2) When you are ready to start work on the examination, that is as soon as the signal has been given, read the instructions to each question booklet, underline any key words or phrases, such as *least, best, outline, describe* and the like. In this way you will tend to answer as requested rather than discover on reviewing your paper that you *listed without describing*, that you selected the *worst* choice rather than the *best* choice, etc.

3) If the examination is of the objective or multiple-choice type – that is, each question will also give a series of possible answers: A, B, C or D, and you are called upon to select the best answer and write the letter next to that answer on your answer paper – it is advisable to start answering each question in turn. There may be anywhere from 50 to 100 such questions in the three or four hours allotted and you can see how much time would be taken if you read through all the questions before beginning to answer any. Furthermore, if you come across a question or group of questions which you know would be difficult to answer, it would undoubtedly affect your handling of all the other questions.

4) If the examination is of the essay type and contains but a few questions, it is a moot point as to whether you should read all the questions before starting to answer any one. Of course, if you are given a choice – say five out of seven and the like – then it is essential to read all the questions so you can eliminate the two which are most difficult. If, however, you are asked to answer all the questions, there may be danger in trying to answer the easiest one first because you may find that you will spend too much time on it. The best technique is to answer the first question, then proceed to the second, etc.

5) Time your answers. Before the exam begins, write down the time it started, then add the time allowed for the examination and write down the time it must be completed, then divide the time available somewhat as follows:
    - If 3-1/2 hours are allowed, that would be 210 minutes. If you have 80 objective-type questions, that would be an average of 2-1/2 minutes per question. Allow yourself no more than 2 minutes per question, or a total of 160 minutes, which will permit about 50 minutes to review.
    - If for the time allotment of 210 minutes there are 7 essay questions to answer, that would average about 30 minutes a question. Give yourself only 25 minutes per question so that you have about 35 minutes to review.

6) The most important instruction is to *read each question* and make sure you know what is wanted. The second most important instruction is to *time yourself properly* so that you answer every question. The third most important instruction is to *answer every question.* Guess if you have to but include something for each question. Remember that you will receive no credit for a blank and will probably receive some credit if you write something in answer to an essay question. If you guess a letter – say "B" for a multiple-choice question – you may have guessed right. If you leave a blank as an answer to a multiple-choice question, the examiners may respect your

feelings but it will not add a point to your score. Some exams may penalize you for wrong answers, so in such cases *only*, you may not want to guess unless you have some basis for your answer.

7) Suggestions
   a. Objective-type questions
      1. Examine the question booklet for proper sequence of pages and questions
      2. Read all instructions carefully
      3. Skip any question which seems too difficult; return to it after all other questions have been answered
      4. Apportion your time properly; do not spend too much time on any single question or group of questions
      5. Note and underline key words – *all, most, fewest, least, best, worst, same, opposite,* etc.
      6. Pay particular attention to negatives
      7. Note unusual option, e.g., unduly long, short, complex, different or similar in content to the body of the question
      8. Observe the use of "hedging" words – *probably, may, most likely,* etc.
      9. Make sure that your answer is put next to the same number as the question
      10. Do not second-guess unless you have good reason to believe the second answer is definitely more correct
      11. Cross out original answer if you decide another answer is more accurate; do not erase until you are ready to hand your paper in
      12. Answer all questions; guess unless instructed otherwise
      13. Leave time for review

   b. Essay questions
      1. Read each question carefully
      2. Determine exactly what is wanted. Underline key words or phrases.
      3. Decide on outline or paragraph answer
      4. Include many different points and elements unless asked to develop any one or two points or elements
      5. Show impartiality by giving pros and cons unless directed to select one side only
      6. Make and write down any assumptions you find necessary to answer the questions
      7. Watch your English, grammar, punctuation and choice of words
      8. Time your answers; don't crowd material

8) Answering the essay question

Most essay questions can be answered by framing the specific response around several key words or ideas. Here are a few such key words or ideas:

M's: manpower, materials, methods, money, management
P's: purpose, program, policy, plan, procedure, practice, problems, pitfalls, personnel, public relations

a. Six basic steps in handling problems:
   1. Preliminary plan and background development
   2. Collect information, data and facts
   3. Analyze and interpret information, data and facts
   4. Analyze and develop solutions as well as make recommendations
   5. Prepare report and sell recommendations
   6. Install recommendations and follow up effectiveness

b. Pitfalls to avoid
   1. *Taking things for granted* – A statement of the situation does not necessarily imply that each of the elements is necessarily true; for example, a complaint may be invalid and biased so that all that can be taken for granted is that a complaint has been registered
   2. *Considering only one side of a situation* – Wherever possible, indicate several alternatives and then point out the reasons you selected the best one
   3. *Failing to indicate follow up* – Whenever your answer indicates action on your part, make certain that you will take proper follow-up action to see how successful your recommendations, procedures or actions turn out to be
   4. *Taking too long in answering any single question* – Remember to time your answers properly

EXAMINATION SECTION

INTRODUCTION TO READING COMPREHENSION

The reading-comprehension question is now a universally accepted ingredient in aptitude, intelligence, general and mental ability, and achievement tests.

By its very nature, it is the most difficult of the question-types to comprehend and to cope with successfully, and, accordingly, it is usually weighted more heavily than all other questions on these examinations.

For the most part, tests of general aptitude and/or achievement draw the reading selections or *passages* from all the disciplines – literature, social studies, science, mathematics, music, art, etc. The student is not expected to, nor does he need to, have knowledge or proficiency in these fields. Rather, he is being tested on his understanding or his comprehension of the meaning of the specific passages presented, the theory being that his mental ability will be best tested by his reading power, not by his training or acquired knowledge in the different areas, since it may be reasonably expected that such training and/or knowledge will differ for many reasons among the candidates. All the information and material needed for answering the questions are, therefore, imbedded in the passages themselves. The power or skill of the student, then, is to be shown in the degree to which he succeeds in finding or inferring the answers to the questions from the information given in the reading material.

Historically, many colleges and universities, leaning on the theory of transfer of training, regard the reading comprehension factor as perhaps the most important of all in measuring scholastic aptitude since, according to this view, the ability to read with understanding and to go on from this point, is basic to all college and graduate work and research.

The factor of reading ability is a complex one which may be tested and measured at several discrete levels.

The easiest type of reading question is that which tests understanding of the material to be read – to list facts or details as described in the passage, to explain the meanings of words or phrases used, to clarify references, etc.

The next stage of difficulty is reached when the student is confronted with questions designed to show his ability to interpret and to analyze the material to be read, e.g., to discover the central thought of the passage, to ascertain the mood or point of view of the author, to note contradictions, etc.

The third stage consists of the ability to apply the principles and/or opinions expressed in the article, e.g., to surmise the recommendations that the writer may be expected to make later on or to formulate his stand on related issues.

The final and highest point is reached when the student is called upon to evaluate what he has read – to agree with or to differ with the point of view of the writer, to accept or to refute the evidences or methods employed, to judge the efficacy or the inappropriateness of different proposals, etc.

All these levels will be tested on the reading section of the Examination.

SUGGESTIONS FOR ANSWERING READING COMPREHENSION QUESTIONS

1. How is the candidate to proceed to answer the reading comprehension questions? First, scan the passage quickly, trying to gather at a glance the general import. Then, read the passage carefully and critically, underlining with a pencil what are apparently leading phrases and concepts.

Finally, read each question carefully, and seek the answer in definite parts - sentences, clauses, phrases, figures of speech, adverbs, adjectives, etc. - in the text of the passage.

2. Be sure to answer the questions only on the basis of the passage, and not from any other source. Answers may not be directly found in the text.

For the more difficult reading questions, answers are usually to be inferred or derived from the sense of one or more sentences, clauses, and even paragraphs.

3. Do not expect to find the bases for the answers in sequential parts of the textual material. The difficulty of questions is increased when the candidate is required to skip from one part of the passage to another without any order, i.e., question 1 may have its root in the last sentence of the paragraph, let us say, and question 5 may be based upon the second sentence, for example. This is a method of increasing the difficulty of the research and investigation required of the candidate.

4. When the question refers to a specific line, sentence, paragraph, or quotation, be sure to find this reference and to re-read it thoroughly. The answer to such a question is almost certain to be, found in or near this reference in the passage.

5. Time for the reading question is limited, as it is for the examination as a whole. In other words, one must work speedily as well as effectively. The candidate, in seeking the answers to the reading questions, is not expected to go through all of the items in the thorough way presented in the sample questions above. That is, he has only to suit himself. It suffices, in order to attain to the right answer, to note mentally the basis for the answer in the text. There is no need to annotate your answer or to write out reasons for your answer. What we have attempted to do in the samples is to show that there is a definite and logical attack on this type of question, which, principally, consists of careful, critical reading, research and investigation, and evaluation of the material. One must learn to arrive at the correct answer through this process rather than through hit or miss tactics or guessing. There is no reading comprehension question, logically or fairly devised, which cannot be answered by the candidate provided he goes about this task in a systematic, sustained manner.

6. The candidate may be assisted by this advanced technique. Often, the general sense of the passage when fully captured, rather than specific parts in the passage, will lead to the correct answer. Therefore, it is most important that the candidate read the passage for total meaning first. This type of general understanding will be most helpful in answering those questions which have no specific background in the text but, rather, must be inferred from what has been read.

7. Beware of the following pitfalls:

a. The categorical statement - You can almost be sure that any answer which uses the words solely, wholly, always, never, at all times, forever, etc., is wrong.

b. The too-easy answer - When the question appears to be so simple that it can be answered almost word for word by reference to the text, be particularly on your guard. You will, probably, find that the language of the question may have been inverted or changed or that some important word has been added or omitted, so that you are being tested for alertness and attention to details. For example, if, in a passage, a comparison is made between Country A and Country B, and you are told that Country A has twice the area of Country B, and the question contains an item which states that *it is clear that the area of Country B is greater than Country A*, note how easily you can be beguiled into accepting this statement as true.

c. Questions requiring that the candidate show his understanding of the main point of a passage, e.g., to state the central theme, or to suggest a worthy title, must be answered on that basis alone. You may be sure that other worthy possibilities are available, but you should examine your choice from the points of view of both appropriateness and breadth. For the most part, answers that are ruled out will contain one, but not both, of these characteristics.

d. Make up your mind now that some, but not all, of the material in the various passages in the reading comprehension questions will be useful for finding the answer. Sometimes, passages are made purposely long to heighten the difficulty and to further confuse the harried candidates. However, do not disregard any of the textual material without first having given it a thorough reading.

e. If the question requires that you give the writer's opinion or feelings or possible future action, do just that, and do not substitute your own predilections or antidotes. Similarly, do not make inferences if there exists in the text a clear-cut statement of facts. Base your answer, preferably, on the facts; make inferences or assumptions when they are called for, or as necessary.

f. Do not expect the passages to deal with your subject field(s) alone. The passages offered will illustrate all the academic areas. While interest is a major factor in attaining to success, resolve now that you are going to wade through all the passages, in a thorough way, be they science or mathematics or economics or art. Unfamiliarity with a subject is no excuse on this type of test since the answers are to be based upon the reading passage alone.

In corollary fashion, should you encounter a passage dealing with a field with which you are familiar, do not permit your special knowledge to play a part in your answer. Answer only on the basis of the passage, as directed.

g. The hardest type of reading question is the one in which the fifth choice presented is *none of these*. Should this phrase prove to be the correct answer, it would require a thorough, albeit rapid, examination of ALL the possibilities. This, of course, is time consuming and often frustrating.

h. A final word of advice at this point. On the examination, leave the more difficult reading questions for the end. Try to answer those of lesser difficulty first. In this way, you will leave yourself maximum time for the really difficult part of the examination.

THE READING COMPREHENSION QUESTION ON THE GED TESTS

What has been said above has prime importance for, and application to, the examinations in the areas of social studies, natural sciences, and literary materials, respectively, as all of these tests are posed in the form of reading comprehension. That is, they consist of a selection of passages from the fields of social studies, natural sciences, and literary materials, respectively, at the high school level, and a number of questions testing the examinee's ability to comprehend and interpret the content of each passage.

As an entity, these tests purpose to determine the student's ability to interpret and to evaluate reading materials representative of those that he will have to read and study in his later school work. By means of this type of test, the student is called upon to demonstrate an expansive background of basic knowledge for it is obvious that a person's ability to interpret and evaluate printed information relative to any special subject depends for the most part upon how much he has already imbibed of the subject and the broad areas from which it has been selected. If the student possesses a wide background, he will be more likely to answer correctly the questions which call for a direct interpretation of the reading selection. A test of this type will thus require that an integrated body of knowledge be applied to particular problems, at the same time not placing any undue reward upon the form or manner in which the candidate's principles have evolved and not penalize him unduly for lack of ability to offer up any particular fact or set of facts where, in truth, another would serve the same general purpose.

These tests, then, are well suited for the task of determining the depth and power of the student's resources of substantial knowledge in the field tested. But the primary reason for using this type of test in this five-test battery is its particular efficacy and felicity in measuring and evaluating the generalized intellectual skills and abilities so necessary for the student for successful school work. These skills and abilities encompass the important aims of detecting errors and inconsistencies in logic; developing and applying generalizations; determining the adequacy of evidence; drawing inferences from data; noting implicit assumptions; searching out meanings not explicitly stated; forming value judgments; recognizing as such appeals to the emotions rather than to the intellect; perceiving and turning away the blandishments of the propagandists; detecting bias; and habituating oneself to the forms and methods of critical thinking.

READING COMPREHENSION
COMMENTARY

Questions on reading comprehension – the ability to understand and interpret written materials – are now universal, staple parts of almost all aptitude and achievement tests, as well as tests of general and mental ability.

By its very nature, the reading comprehension question is the most difficult of the question-types to cope with successfully, and, accordingly, it is usually weighted more heavily (assigned more credits) than other questions.

Generally, tests of aptitude and/or achievement derive their reading selections ("passages") from the several disciplines – art, biology, chemistry, economics, education, engineering, history, literature, mathematics, music, philosophy, physics, political science, psychology, and sociology. Thus, the student or applicant is not being tested for specific knowledge of, or proficiency in, these areas. Rather, he is being tested on his understanding and comprehension of the meaning of the materials contained in the specific passages presented, the theory being that his mental ability will be best tested by his reading power, not by his training or acquired knowledge in the different fields, since it may be reasonably expected that such training and/or knowledge will differ among the candidates for a variety of reasons. The great equalizing element is the reading comprehension test. Therefore, all the information and material needed for answering the questions are imbedded in the passages themselves. *The power or skill or ability of the testtaker, then, is to be shown in the extent and degree to which he succeeds in making the correct answers to the questions in the reading passages.*

Historically, many colleges and universities, leaning on the theory of transfer of training, regard the reading comprehension factor as, perhaps the most important of all criteria in measuring scholastic aptitude since, according to this view, the ability to read with understanding and to go on from this point, is basic to all academic professional, graduate, and research work.

Let us examine just what reading comprehension means in the context described above and analyze its basic components.

The factor of reading ability is a complex one which may be tested and measured at several discrete levels of ability.

Comparatively, the easiest type of reading question is that which tests understanding of the material to be read – to list facts or details as described in the passage, to explain the meanings of words or phrases used, to clarify references, etc.

The next level of difficulty is reached when the student is confronted with questions designed to show his ability to interpret and to analyze the material to be read, e.g., to discover the central thought of the passage, to ascertain the mood or point of view of the author, to note contradictions, etc.

The third stage consists of the ability to apply the principles and/or opinions expressed in the article, e.g., to surmise the recommendations that the writer may be expected to make later on or to formulate his stand on related issues.

The final and highest point is attained when the student is called upon to evaluate what he has read – agree with or to differ with the point of view of the writer, to accept or to refute the evidences or methods employed, to judge the efficacy or the inappropriateness of different proposals, etc.

All these levels will be broached and tested in this reading section.

SAMPLE PASSAGE - QUESTIONS AND ANSWERS

PASSAGE

(1) Our ignorance of the complex subject of social insurance was and remains colossal. (2) For years American business leaders delighted in maligning the British social insurance schemes. (3) Our industrialists condemned them without ever finding out what they were about. (4) Even our universities displayed no interest. (5) Contrary to the interest in this subject taken by organized labor abroad, our own labor movement bitterly opposed the entire program of social insurance up to a few years ago. (6) Since the success of any reform depends largely upon a correct public understanding of the principles involved, the adoption of social insurance measures presented peculiar difficulties for the United States under our Federal type of government of limited powers, our constitutional and judicial handicaps, our long conditioning to individualism, the traditional hostility to social reform by both capital and labor, the general inertia, and our complete lack of trained administrative personnel without which even the best law can be ineffective. (7) Has not bitter experience taught us that far more important than the passage of a law, which is at best only a declaration of intention, is a ready public opinion prepared to enforce it?

1. According to this writer, what attitude have we shown in this country toward social insurance? 1._

   A. We have been extremely doubtful that it will work, but have been willing to give it a chance.
   B. We have opposed it on the grounds of a careful study of its defects.
   C. We have shown an unintelligent and rather blind antagonism toward it.
   D. We have been afraid that it would not work under our type of government.
   E. We have resented it because of the extensive propaganda in favor of it.

2. To what does the phrase, “our long conditioning to individualism,” refer? 2._

   A. Our habit of depending upon ourselves
   B. Our increasing dependence on the Federal Government
   C. Our long established distrust of “big business”
   D. Our policies of high protective tariff
   E. Our unwillingness to accept reforms

3. Which of these ideas is expressed in this passage? 3.____

A. The surest way to cure a social evil is to get people to pass a law against it.
B. Legislation alone cannot effect social reforms.
C. The American people are seriously uninformed about all social problems.
D. Our type of government makes social reform practically impossible.
E. Capital and labor retard social progress.

ANALYSIS

These are the steps you must take to answer the questions:

First, scan the passage quickly, trying to gather at a glance the general import.

Then, read the passage carefully and critically, underlining with a pencil, what are apparently leading phrases and concepts.

Next, read each question carefully, and seek the answer in definite parts – sentences, clauses, phrases, figures of speech, adverbs, adjectives, etc. – in the text of the passage.

Finally, select the one answer which best answers the question, that is, it *best* matches what the paragraph says or is *best* supported by something in the passage.

The passage is concerned with the advent of social insurance to the United States. The author makes several points in this connection:

1. Our gross ignorance of, and lack of interest in, the subject.
2. The bitter opposition to social insurance in this country, particularly, of organized labor.
3. Special and augmented difficulties in the United States in respect to this area; enumeration of these factors.
4. The ultimate, certain method of achieving reform.

Having firmly encompassed the central meaning and basic contents of the passage, let us now proceed to examine each of the stated questions and proposed answers.

Question 1. According to this writer, what attitude have we shown in this country toward social insurance?

A. We have been extremely doubtful that it will work, but have been willing to give it a chance.
Sentences 1, 2, 3, 4, 5 drastically negate the second clause of this statement ("but we have been willing to give it a chance").
B. We have opposed it on the grounds of a careful study of its defects.
This statement is completely refuted by sentences 2 and 3.
C. We have shown an unintelligent and rather blind antagonism toward it.
Just as A is fully denied by sentences 1-5, so these sentences fully Affirm the validity of this statement.
D. We have been afraid that it would not work under our type of government.
This is one – and only one – of the several difficulties facing the success of social insurance. Thus, this answer is only *partially* true.
E. We have resented it because of the extensive propaganda in favor of it.
Quite the contrary. Again, see sentences 1-5.

Looking back, you now see that the one suggested answer of the five (5) offered that BEST answers the question is item C, We have shown an unintelligent and rather blind antagonism toward it. The CORRECT answer, then, is C.

Question 2. To what does the phrase, "our long conditioning to individualism," refer?

A. Our habit of depending upon ourselves.

When a phrase is quoted from the text, as in this question, we should immediately locate it, review the context, and then consider it *in the light of the meaning of the passage as a whole.*

We find the quoted phrase in long sentence 6, beginning "Since the success..."

A is clearly the answer to question 2.

Items B, C, D, E have little or no merit with reference to the meaning of the quoted phrase within the passage, and are, therefore, to be discarded as possible answers.

Question 3. Which of these ideas is expressed in this passage?

A. The surest way to cure a social evil is to get people to pass a law against it.

This is clearly refuted by the last sentence, "Has not bitter experience... it?"

B. Legislation alone cannot effect social reforms.

This is just as clearly supported by this same last sentence.

C. The American people are seriously uninformed about all social problems.

There is no evidence in the passage to support this statement.

D. Our type of government makes social reform practically impossible.

Our democratic form of government does present serious handicaps to social reform, as stated in the next-to-last sentence, but does not make social reform "practically impossible."

E. Capital and labor retard social progress.

American business leaders and the labor movement both opposed social *insurance.* They did not, however, retard social *progress.*

SUGGESTIONS FOR ANSWERING THE READING COMPREHENSION QUESTION

1. Be sure to answer the questions only on the basis of the passage, and not from any other source, unless specifically directed to do otherwise.
2. Note that the answers may not be found directly in the text. For the more difficult reading questions, answers are generally to be *inferred* or *derived* from the sense of one or more sentences, clauses, and even paragraphs.
3. Do not expect to find the bases for the answers in sequential parts of the textual material. The difficulty of questions is increased when the candidate is required to skip from one part of the passage to another without any order, i.e., Question 1 may have its root in the last sentence of the paragraph, let us say, and Question 5 may be based upon the second sentence, for example. This is a method of increasing the difficulty of the research and investigation required of the candidate.
4. When the question refers to a specific line, sentence, paragraph, or quotation, be sure to find this reference and to re-read it thoroughly. The answer to such a question is almost certain to be found in or near this reference in the passage.
5. Time for the reading question is limited, as it is for the examination as a whole. In other words, one must work speedily as well as effectively. The candidate, in seeking the answers to the reading questions, is not expected to go through all of the items in the thorough way presented in the sample questions above. That is, he has only to suit himself. It suffices, in order to attain to the right answer, to note mentally the basis for the answer in the text. There is no need to annotate your answer or to write out reasons for your answer. What we have attempted to do in the samples is to show that there is a definite and logical attack on this type of question, which, principally, consists of careful, critical reading, research and investigation, and evaluation of the material. One must learn to arrive at the correct answer through this process rather than through hit-or-miss tactics or guessing. There is no reading comprehension question, logically or fairly devised, which cannot be answered by the candidate provided he goes about this task in a systematic, sustained manner.
6. The candidate may be assisted by this advanced technique. Often, the general sense of the passage when fully captured, rather than specific parts in the passage, will lead to the correct answer. Therefore, it is most important that the candidate read the passage for total meaning first. This type of general understanding will be most helpful in answering those questions which have no specific background in the text but, rather, must be inferred from what has been read.

7. Beware of the following pitfalls:

   A. The categorical statement. – You can almost be sure that any answer which uses the words solely, wholly, always, never, at all times, forever, etc., is wrong.

   B. The too-easy answer. – When the question appears to be so simple that it can be answered almost word for word by reference to the text, be particularly on your guard. You will, probably, find that the language of the question may have been inverted or changed or that some important word has been added or omitted, so that you are being tested for alertness and attention to details. For example, if, in a passage, a comparison is made between Country A and Country B, and you are told that Country A has twice the area of Country B, and the question contains an item which states that "it is clear that the area of Country B is greater than Country A," note how easily you can be beguiled into accepting this statement as true.

C. Questions requiring that the candidate show his understanding of the main point of a passage, e.g., to state the central theme, or to suggest a worthy title, must be answered on that basis alone. You may be sure that other worthy possibilities are available, but you should examine your choice from the points of view of both appropriateness and breadth. For the most part, answers that are ruled out will contain one, but not both of these characteristics.

D. Make up your mind now that some, but not all, of the material in the various passages in the reading comprehension questions will be useful for finding the answer. Sometimes, passages are made purposely long to increase the difficulty and to further confuse the harried candidates. However, do not disregard any of the textual material without first having given it a thorough reading.

E. If the question requires that you give the writer's opinion or feelings on possible future action, do just that, and do not substitute your own predilections or antidotes. Similarly, do not make inferences if there exists in the text a clear-cut statement of facts. Base your answer, preferably, on the facts; make inferences or assumptions when they are called for, or as necessary.

F. Do not expect the passages to deal with your subject field(s) alone. The passages offered will illustrate all the academic areas. While interest is a major factor in attaining to success, resolve now that you are going to wade through all the passages, in a thorough way, be they science or mathematics or economics or art. Unfamiliarity with a subject is no excuse on this type of test since the answers are to be based upon the reading passage alone.

In corollary fashion, should you encounter a passage dealing with a field with which you are familiar, do not permit your special knowledge to play a part in your answer. Answer only on the basis of the passage, as directed.

G. The hardest type of reading question is the one in which the fifth choice presented is "none of these." Should this phrase prove to be the correct answer, it would require a thorough, albeit rapid, examination of ALL the possibilities. This, of course, is time consuming and often frustrating.

H. A final word of advice at this point. On the examination, leave the more difficult reading questions for the end. Try to answer those of lesser difficulty first. In this way, you will leave yourself maximum time for the really difficult part of the examination.

In accordance with the special challenge of the reading comprehension question, ten (10) selected passages, varying in subject matter, style, length, and form, are presented for solution by the candidate. However, the passages are all alike in one respect: they extend to the highest ranges of difficulty.

READING COMPREHENSION
UNDERSTANDING AND INTERPRETING WRITTEN MATERIAL
STRATEGIES

Surveying Passages, Sentences as Cues

While individual readers develop unique reading styles and skills, there are some known strategies which can assist any reader in improving his or her reading comprehension and performance on the reading subtest. These strategies include understanding how single paragraphs and entire passages are structured, how the ideas in them are ordered, and how the author of the passage has connected these ideas in a logical and sequential way for the reader.

The section that follows highlights the importance of reading a passage through once for meaning, and provides instruction on careful reading for context cues within the sentences before and after the missing word.

SURVEY THE ENTIRE PASSAGE

To get a sense of the topic and the organization of ideas in a passage, it is important to survey each passage initially in its entirety and to identify the main idea. (The first sentence of a paragraph usually states the main idea.) Do not try to fill in the blanks initially. The purpose of surveying a passage is to prepare for the more careful reading which will follow. You need a sense of the big picture before you start to fill in the details; for example, a quick survey of the passage on page 11, indicates that the topic is the early history of universities. The paragraphs are organized to provide information on the origin of the first universities, the associations formed by teachers and students, the early curriculum, and graduation requirements.

READ PRECEDING SENTENCES CAREFULLY

The missing words in a passage cannot be determined by reading and understanding only the sentences in which the deletions occur. Information from the sentences which precede or follow can provide important cues to determine the correct choice. For example, if you read the first sentence from the passage about universities which contains a blank, you will notice that all the alternatives make sense if this one sentence is read in isolation:

Nobody actually ______ them.

A. started
B. guarded
C. blamed
D. compared
E. remembered

The only way that you can make the correct word choice is to read the preceding sentences. In the excerpt below, notice that the first sentence tells the reader what the passage will be about: how universities developed. A key word in the first sentence is *emerged,* which is closely related in meaning to one of the five choices for the first blank. The second sentence explains the key word, *emerged,* by pointing out that we have no historical record of a decree or a date indicating when the first university was established. Understanding the ideas in the first two sentences makes it possible to select the correct word for the blank. Look at the sentence with the deleted word in the context of the preceding sentences and think about why you are now able to make the correct choice.

> The first universities emerged at the end of the 11th century and beginning of the 12th. These institutions were not founded on any particular date or created by any formal action. Nobody actually ______ them.
>
> A. started B. guarded
> C. blamed D. compared
> E. remembered

Started is the best choice because it fits the main idea of the passage and is closely related to the key word *emerged.*

READ THE SENTENCE WHICH FOLLOWS TO VERIFY YOUR CHOICE

The sentences which follow the one from which a word has been deleted may also provide cues to the correct choice. For example, look at an excerpt from the passage about universities again, and consider how the sentence which follows the one with the blank helps to reinforce the choice of the word, *started.*

> The first universities emerged at the end of the llth century and the beginning of the 12th. These institutions were not founded on any particular date or created by any formal action. Nobody actually ______ them. Instead, they developed gradually in places like Paris, Oxford, and Bologna, where scholars had long been teaching students.
>
> A. started B. guarded
> C. blamed D. compared
> E. remembered

The words, *developed gradually,* mean the same as the key word, *emerged.* The signal word, *instead,* helps to distinguish the difference between starting on a specific date as a result of some particular act or event and emerging over a period of time as a result of various factors.

Here is another example of how the sentence which follows the one from which a word is deleted might help you decide which of two good alternatives is the correct choice. This excerpt is from the practice passage about bridges (page 11).

> Bridges are built to allow a continuous flow of highway and railway traffic across water lying in their paths. But engineers cannot forget that river traffic, too, is essential to our economy. The role of ______ is important. To keep these vessels moving freely, bridges are built big enough, when possible, to let them pass underneath.
>
> A. wind B. boats
> C. weight D. wires
> E. experiences

After the first two sentences, the reader may be uncertain about the direction the writer intended to take in the rest of the paragraph. If the writer intended to continue the paragraph with information concerning how engineers make choices about the relative importance and requirements of land traffic and river traffic, *experience* might be the appropriate choice for the missing word. However, the sentence following the one in which the deletion occurs makes it clear that *boats* is the correct choice. It provides the synonym *vessels,* which in the noun phrase *these vessels* must refer back to the previous sentence or sentences. The phrase *to let them pass underneath* also helps make it clear that *boats* is the appropriate choice. *Them* refers back to *these vessels* which, in turn, refers back to *boats* when the word *boats* is placed in the previous sentence. Thus, the reader may use these cohesive ties (the pronoun referents) to verify the final choice.

Even when the text following a sentence with a deletion is not necessary to choose the best alternative, it may be helpful in other ways. Specifically, complete sentences provide important transitions into a related topic which is developed in the rest of the paragraph or in the next paragraph of the same passage. For example, the first paragraph in the passage about universities ends with a sentence which introduces the term *guilds*: *But, over time, they joined together to form guilds.* Prior to this sentence, information about the slow emergence of universities and about how independently scholars had acted was introduced. The next paragraph begins with two sentences about guilds in general. Someone who had not read the last sentence in the first paragraph might have missed the link between guilds and scholars and universities and, thus, might have been unnecessarily confused.

Cohesive Ties As Cues

Sentences in a paragraph may be linked together by several devices called cohesive ties. Attention to these ties may provide further cues about missing words. This section will describe the different types of cohesive ties and show how attention to them can help you to select the correct word.

PERSONAL PRONOUNS

Personal pronouns (e.g., he, she, they, it, its) are often used in adjoining sentences to refer back to an already mentioned person, place, thing, or idea. The word to which the pronoun refers is called the antecedent.

Tools used in farm work changed very slowly from ancient times to the eighteenth century, and the changes were minor. Since the eighteenth century *they* have changed quickly and dramatically.

The word *they* refers back to *tools* in the example above.

In the examination reading subtest, a deleted word sometimes occurs in a sentence in which the sentence subject is a pronoun that refers back to a previously mentioned noun. You must correctly identify the referent for the particular pronoun in order to interpret the sentence and select the correct answer. Here is an example from the passage about bridges.

An ingenious engineer designed the bridge so that it did not have to be raised above traffic. Instead it was ______.

A. burned
B. emptied
C. secured
D. shared
E. lowered

Q. What is the antecedent of *it* in both cases in the example?

A. The antecedent, of course, is *bridge*.

DEMONSTRATIVE PRONOUNS

Demonstrative pronouns (e.g., this, that, these) are also used to refer to a specific, previously mentioned noun. They may occur alone as noun replacements, or they may accompany and modify nouns.

I like jogging, swimming, and tennis. *These* are the only sports I enjoy.

In the sentence above, the word *these* is a replacement noun. However, demonstrative pronouns may also occur as adjectives modifying nouns.

I like jogging, swimming, and tennis. *These* sports are the only ones I enjoy.

The word *these* in the example above is an adjective modifier. The word *these* in each of the two previous examples refers to *jogging, swimming,* and *tennis.*

Here is an example from the passage about universities on page 12.

Undergraduates took classes in Greek philosophy, Latin grammar, arithmetic, music, and astronomy. These were the only ______ available.

A. rooms
B. subjects
C. clothes
D. pens
E. company

Q. Which word is a noun replacement?
A. The word *these* is the replacement noun for *Greek philosophy, Latin grammar, arithmetic, music,* and *astronomy.*

Here is another example from the same passage.

The concept of a fixed program of study leading to a degree first evolved in Medieval Europe. This ______ had not appeared before.

A. idea
B. desk
C. library
D. capital

Q. What is the antecedent of *this*?

A. The antecedent is *the concept of a fixed program of study leading to a degree.*

COMPARATIVE ADJECTIVES AND ADVERBS

When comparative adjectives or adverbs (e.g., so, such, better, more) occur, they refer to something else in the passage, otherwise a comparison could not be made.

The hotels in the city were all full; so were the motels and boarding houses.

Q. To what in the first sentence does the word *so* refer?
A. *So* tells us to compare the *motels* and *boarding houses* to the *hotels in the city.*

Q. In what way are the *hotels, motels,* and *boarding houses* similar to each other?

A. The *hotels, motels,* and *boarding houses* are similar in that they were all *full.*

Look at an example from the passage about universities.

Guilds were groups of tradespeople, somewhat akin to modern trade unions. In the Middle Ages, all the crafts had such

A. taxes
B. secrets
C. products
D. problems
E. organizations

Q. To what in the first sentence does the word *such* refer?
A. *Such* refers to *groups of tradespeople.*

SUBSTITUTIONS

Substitution is another form of cohesive tie. A substitution occurs when one linguistic item (e.g., a noun) is replaced by another. Sometimes the substitution provides new or contrasting information. The substitution is not identical to the original, or antecedent, idea. A frequently occurring substitution involves the use of *one.* A noun substitution may involve another member of the same class as the original one.

My car is falling apart. I need a new one.

Q. What in the first sentence is replaced in the second sentence with *one?*
A. *One* is a substitute for the specific car mentioned in the first sentence. The contrast comes from the fact that the *new one* isn't the writer's current car.

The substitution may also pinpoint a specific member of a general class.

1. There are many unusual courses available at the university this summer. The *one* I am taking is called *Death and Dying.*
2. There are many unusual courses available at the university this summer. *Some* have never been offered before.

Q. In these examples, what is the general class in the first sentence that is replaced by *one* and by *some*?
A. In both cases the words *one* and *some* replace *many unusual* courses.

SYNONYMS

Synonyms are words that have similar meaning. In the examination reading subtest, a synonym of a deleted word is sometimes found in one of the sentences before and/or after the sentence with the deletion. Examine the following excerpt from the passage about bridges again.

But engineers cannot forget that river traffic, too, is essential to our economy. The role of ______ is important. To keep these vessels moving freely, bridges are built high enough, when possible, to let them pass underneath.

A. wind
B. boats
C. weight
D. wires
E. experience

Q Can you identify synonyms in the sentences, before and after the sentence containing the deletion, which are cues to the correct deleted word?

A. If you identified the correct words, you probably noticed that *river traffic* is not exactly a synonym, since it is a slightly more general term than the word *boats* (the correct choice). But the word *vessels* is a direct synonym. Demonstrative pronouns (this, that, these, those) are sometimes used as modifiers for synonymous nouns in sentences which follow those containing deletions. The word *these* in *these vessels* is the demonstrative pronoun (modifier) for the synonymous noun *vessels.*

ANTONYMS

Antonyms are words of opposite meaning. In the examination reading subtest passages, antonyms may be cues for missing words. A contrasting relationship, which calls for the use of an antonym, is often signaled by the connective words *instead, however, but,* etc. Look at an excerpt from the passage about bridges.

An ingenious engineer designed the bridge so that it did not have to be raised above traffic. Instead it was ______.

A. burned
B. emptied
C. secured
D. shared
E. lowered

Q. Can you identify an antonym in the first sentence for one of the five alternatives?

A. The word *raised* is an antonym for the word *lowered.*

SUPERORDINATE-SUBORDINATE WORDS

In the examination reading subtest, a passage sometimes contains a general term which provides a cue that a more specific term is the appropriate alternative. At other times, the passage may contain a specific term which provides cues that a general term is the appropriate alternative for a particular deletion. The general and more specific words are said to have superordinate-subordinate relationships.

Look at example 1 below. The more specific word *boy* in the first sentence serves as the antecedent for the more general word *child* in the second sentence. In example 2, the relationship is reversed. In both examples, the words *child* and *boy* reflect a superordinate-subordinate relationship.

1. The *boy* climbed the tree. Then the *child* fell.
2. The *child* climbed the tree. Then the *boy* fell.

In the practice passage about bridges on page 11, the phrase *river traffic* is a general term that is superordinate to the alternative *boats* (item 1). Later in the passage about bridges the following sentences also contain superordinate-subordinate words:

A lift bridge was desired, but there were wartime shortages of steel and machinery needed for the towers. It was hard to find enough ______.

A. work
B. material
C. time
D. power
E. space

Q. Can you identify two words in the first sentence that are specific examples for the correct response in the second sentence?
A. Of course, the words *steel* and *machinery* are the specific examples for the more general term *material.*

WORDS ASSOCIATED BY ENTAILMENT

Sometimes the concept described by one word within the context of the passage entails, or implies, the concept described by another word. For example, consider again item 7 in the practice passage about bridges. Notice how the follow-up sentence to item 7 provides a cue to the correct response.

An ingenious engineer designed the bridge so that it did not have to be raised above traffic. Instead it was _______. It could be submerged seven meters below the surface of the river.

A. burned
B. emptied
C. secured
D. shared
E. lowered

Q. What word in the sentence after the blank implies the concept of an alternative?
A. *Submerged* implies *lowered.* The concept of submerging something implies the idea of lowering the object beneath the surface of the water.

WORDS ASSOCIATED BY PART-WHOLE RELATIONSHIPS

Words may be related because they involve part of a whole and the whole itself; for example, *nose* and *face.* Words may also be related because they involve two parts of the same whole; for example, *radiator* and *muffler* both refer to parts of a car.

The captain of the ship was nervous. The storm was becoming worse and worse. The hardened man paced the _______.

A. floor
B. hall
C. deck
D. court

Q. Which choice has a part-whole relationship with a word in the sentences above?
A. A *deck.* is a part of a *ship.* Therefore, *deck* has a part-whole relationship with *ship.*

CONJUNCTIVE AND CONNECTIVE WORDS AND PHRASES

Conjunctions or connectives are words or phrases that connect parts of sentences or parts of a passage to each other. Their purpose is to help the reader understand the logical and conceptual relationships between ideas and events within a passage. Examples of these words and phrases include coordinate conjunctions (e.g., and, but, yet), subordinate conjunctions (e.g., because, although, since, after), and other connective words and phrases (e,g, too, also, on the other hand, as a result).

Listed below are types of logical relationships expressed by conjunctive, or connective words. Also listed are examples of words used to cue relationships to the reader.

Additive and comparative words and phrases: and, in addition to, too, also, furthermore, similarly

Adversative and contrastive words and phrases: yet, though, only, but, however, instead, rather, on the other hand, in contrast, conversely

Causal words or phrases: so, therefore, because, as a result, if...then, unless, except, in that case, under the circumstances

Temporal words and phrases: before, after, when, while, initially, lastly, finally, until.

<u>Examples</u>

1. I enjoy fast-paced sports like tennis and volleyball, but my brother prefers _______ sports.

A. running
B. slower
C. team
D. active

Q. What is the connective word that tells you to look for a contrast relationship between the two clauses?
A The connective word *but* signals that a contrast relationship exists between the two parts of the sentence.

Q. Of the four options, what is the best choice for the blank?
A The word *slower* is the best response here.

2. The child stepped to close to the edge of the brook. As a result, he _______ in.

A. fell
B. waded
C. ran
D. jumped

Q. What is the connective phrase that links the two sentences?
A. The connective phrase *as a result* links the two sentences.

Q. Of the four relationships of words and phrases listed previously, what kind of relationship between the two sentences does the connective phrase in the example signal to the reader?
A. The phrase *as a result* signals that a cause and effect relationship exists between the two sentences.

Q. Identify the correct response which makes the second sentence reflect the cause and effect relationship.
A. The correct response is *fell.*

Understanding connectives is very important to success on the examination reading sub-test. Sentences with deletions are often very closely related to adjacent sentences in meaning, and the relationship is often signaled by connective words or phrases. Here is an example from the practice passage about universities.

> At first, these tutors had not been associated with one another. Rather, they had been _______. But, over time, they joined together to form guilds.
>
> A. curious
> B. poor
> C. religious
> D. ready
> E. independent

Q. Identify the connective and contrastive words and phrases in the example.

A. *At first* and *over time* are connective phrases that set up temporal progression. *Rather* and *but* are contrastive items. The use of *rather* in the sentence with the deletion tells the reader that the missing word has to convey a meaning in contrast to *associated with one another.* (Notice also that *rather* occurs after a negative statement.) The use of *but* in the sentence after the one with the deletion indicates that the deleted word in the previous sentence has to reflect a meaning that contrasts with *joined together.* Thus, the reader is given two substantial cues to the meaning of the missing word. *Independent* is the only choice that meets the requirement for contrastive meaning.

SAMPLE QUESTIONS

DIRECTIONS: There are two passages on the following pages. In each passage some words are missing. Wherever a word is missing, there is a blank line with a number on it. Below the passage you will find the same number and five words. Choose the word that makes the best sense in the blank. You may not be sure of the answer to a question until you read the sentences that come after the blank, so be sure to read enough to answer the questions. As you work on these passages, you will find that the second passage is harder to read than the first. Answer as many questions as you can.

Bridges are built to allow a continuous flow of highway and railway traffic across water lying in their paths. But engineers cannot forget that river traffic, too, is essential to our economy.The role of ___1___ is important. To keep these vessels moving freely, bridges are built high enough, when possible, to let them pass underneath. Sometimes, however, channels must accommodate very tall ships. It may be uneconomical to build a tall enough bridge. The ___2___ would be too high. To save money, engineers build movable bridges.

In the swing bridge, the middle part pivots or swings open. When the bridge is closed, this section joins the two ends of the bridge, blocking tall vessels. But this section ___3___ . When swung open, it is perpendicular to the ends of the bridge, creating two free channels for river traffic. With swing bridges channel width is limited by the bridge's piers. The largest swing bridge provides only a 75-meter channel. Such channels are sometimes too ___4___ . In such cases, a bascule bridge may be built.

Bascule bridges are drawbridges with two arms that swing upward. They provide an opening as wide as the span. They are also versatile. These bridges are not limited to being fully opened or fully closed. They can be ___5___ in many ways. They can be fixed at different angles to accommodate different vessels.

In vertical lift bridges, the center remains horizontal. Towers at both ends allow the center to be lifted like an elevator. One interesting variation of this kind of bridge was built during World War II. A lift bridge was desired, but there were wartime shortages of the steel and machinery needed for the towers. It was hard to find enough ___6___ . An ingenious engineer designed the bridge so that it did not have to be raised above traffic. Instead it was ___7___ . It could be submerged seven meters below the surface of the river. Ships sailed over it.

1. A. wind B. boats C. experience
D. wires E. experience

2. A. levels B. cost C. standards
D. waves E. deck

3. A. stands B. floods C. wears
D. turns E. supports

4. A. narrow B. rough C. long
D. deep E. straight

5. A. crossed B. approached C. lighted
D. planned E. positioned

6. A. work B. material C. time
D. power E. space

7. A. burned B. emptied C. secured
D. shared E. lowered

The first universities emerged at the end of the 11th century and beginning of the 12th. These institutions were not founded on any particular date or created by any formal action. Nobody actually ___8___ them. Instead, they developed gradually in places like Paris, Oxford, and Bologna, where scholars had long been teaching students. At first, these tutors had not been associated with one another. Rather, they had been ___9___ . But, over time, they joined together to form guilds.

Guilds were groups of tradespeople, somewhat akin to modern unions. In the Middle Ages, all the crafts had such ___10___ . The scholars' guilds built school buildings and evolved an administration which charged fees and set standards for the curriculum. It set prices for members' services and fixed requirements for entering the profession.

Professors were not the only schoolpeople forming associations. In Italy, students joined guilds to which teachers had to swear obedience. The students set strict rules, fining professors for beginning class a minute late. Teachers had to seek their students' permission to marry, and such permission was not always granted. Sometimes the students ___11___ . Even if they said yes, the teacher got only one day's honeymoon.

Undergraduates took classes in Greek philosophy, Latin grammar, arithmetic, music, and astronomy. These were the only ___12___ available. More advanced study was possible in law, medicine, and theology, but one could not earn such postgraduate degrees quickly. It took a long time to ___13___ . Completing the requirements in theology, for example, took at least 13 years.

The concept of a fixed program of study leading to a degree first evolved in medieval Europe. This ___14___ had not appeared before. In earlier academic settings, notions about *meeting requirements* and *graduating* had been absent. Since the Middle Ages, though, we have continued to view education as a set curriculum culminating in a degree.

8. A. started B. guarded C. blamed
   D. compared E. remembered

9. A. curious B. poor C. religious
   D. curious E. independent

10. A. taxes B. secrets C. products
    D. problems E. organizations

11. A. left B. copied C. refused
    D. paid E. prepared

12. A. rooms B. subjects C. clothes
    D. pens E. markets

13. A. add B. answer C. forget
    D. finish E. travel

14. A. idea B. desk C. library
    D. capital E. company

KEY (CORRECT ANSWERS)

1. B
2. B
3. D
4. A
5. E
6. B
7. E
8. A
9. E
10. E
11. C
12. B
13. D
14. A

TESTS IN SENTENCE COMPLETION / 1 BLANK

EXAMINATION SECTION

TEST 1

DIRECTIONS: Each question in this section consists of a sentence in which one word is missing; a blank line indicates where the word has been removed from the sentence. Beneath each sentence are five words, *one* of which is the missing word. You are to select the letter of the missing word by deciding which one of the five words BEST fits in with the meaning of the sentence. *PRINT THE LETTER OF THE CORRECT ANSWER IN THE SPACE AT THE RIGHT.*

1. A man who cannot win honor in his own _______ will have a very small chance of winning it from posterity. 1.____

   A. right B. field C. country D. way E. age

2. The latent period for the contractile response to direct stimulation of the muscle has quite another and shorte value, encompassing only a utilization period. Hence it is that the term *latent period* must be _______ carefully each time that it is used. 2.____

   A. checked B. timed C. introduced
   D. defined E. selected

3. Many television watchers enjoy stories which contain violence. Consequently those television producers who are dominated by rating systems aim to _______ the popular taste. 3.____

   A. raise B. control C. gratify D. ignore E. lower

4. No other man loses so much, so _______, so absolutely, as the beaten candidate for high public office. 4.____

   A. bewilderingly B. predictably C. disgracefully
   D. publicly E. cheerfully

5. Mathematics is the product of thought operating by means of _______ for the purpose of expressing general laws. 5.____

   A. reasoning B. symbols C. words
   D. examples E. science

6. Deductive reasoning is that form of reasoning in which the conclusion must necessarily follow if we accept the premise as true. In deduction, it is _______ the premise to be true and the conclusion false. 6.____

   A. impossible B. inevitable C. reasonable
   D. surprising E. unlikely

7. Because in the administration it hath respect not to the group but to the _______, our form of government is called a democracy. 7.____

   A. courts B. people C. majority
   D. individual E. law

8. Before criticizing the work of an artist one needs to _______ the artist's purpose. 8.___

A. understand B. reveal C. defend
D. correct E. change

9. Their work was commemorative in character and consisted largely of _______ erected upon the occasion of victories. 9.___

A. towers B. tombs C. monuments
D. castles E. fortresses

10. Every good story is carefully contrived: the elements of the story are _______ to fit with one another in order to make an effect on the reader. 10.___

A. read B. learned C. emphasized
D. reduced E. planned

KEY (CORRECT ANSWERS)

1.	E	6.	A
2.	D	7.	D
3.	C	8.	A
4.	D	9.	C
5.	B	10.	E

TEST 2

DIRECTIONS: Each question in this section consists of a sentence in which one word is missing; a blank line indicates where the word has been removed from the sentence. Beneath each sentence are five words, *one* of which is the missing word. You are to select the letter of the missing word by deciding which one of the five words BEST fits in with the meaning of the sentence. *PRINT THE LETTER OF THE CORRECT ANSWER IN THE SPACE AT THE RIGHT.*

1. One of the most prevalent erroneous contentions is that Argentina is a country of ______ agricultural resources and needs only the arrival of ambitious settlers. 1.____

   A. modernized B. flourishing C. undeveloped
   D. waning E. limited

2. The last official statistics for the town indicated the presence of 24,212 Italians, 6,450 Magyars, and 2,315 Germans, which ensures to the ______ a numerical preponderance. 2.____

   A. Germans B. figures C. town D. Magyars E. Italians

3. Precision of wording is necessary in good writing; by choosing words that exactly convey the desired meaning, one can avoid ______. 3.____

   A. duplicity B. incongruity C. complexity
   D. ambiguity E. implications

4. Various civilians of the liberal school in the British Parliament remonstrated that there were no grounds for ______ of French aggression, since the Emperor showed less disposition to augment the navy than had Louis Philippe. 4.____

   A. suppression B. retaliation C. apprehension
   D. concealment E. commencement

5. ______ is as clear and definite as any of our urges; we wonder what is in a sealed letter or what is being said in a telephone booth. 5.____

   A. Envy B. Curiosity C. Knowledge
   D. Communication E. Ambition

6. It is a rarely philosophic soul who can make a ______ the other alternative forever into the limbo of forgotten things. 6.____

   A. mistake B. wish C. change D. choice E. plan

7. A creditor is worse than a master. A master owns only your person, but a creditor owns your ______ as well. 7.____

   A. aspirations B. potentialities C. ideas
   D. dignity E. wealth

8. People ______ small faults, in order to insinuate that they have no great ones. 8.____

   A. create B. display C. confess D. seek E. reject

9. Andrew Jackson believed that wars were inevitable, and to him the length and irregularity of our coast presented a _______ that called for a more than merely passive navy. 9.__

A. defense B. barrier C. provocation
D. vulnerability E. dispute

10. The progressive yearly _______ of the land, caused by the depositing of mud from the river, makes it possible to estimate the age of excavated remains by noting the depth at which they are found below the present level of the valley. 10.__

A. erosion B. elevation C. improvement
D. irrigation E. displacement

KEY (CORRECT ANSWERS)

1. C
2. E
3. D
4. C
5. B
6. D
7. D
8. C
9. D
10. B

TEST 3

DIRECTIONS: Each question in this section consists of a sentence in which one word is missing; a blank line indicates where the word has been removed from the sentence. Beneath each sentence are five words, *one* of which is the missing word. You are to select the letter of the missing word by deciding which one of the five words BEST fits in with the meaning of the sentence. *PRINT THE LETTER OF THE CORRECT ANSWER IN THE SPACE AT THE RIGHT.*

1. The judge exercised commendable _______ dismissing the charge against the prisoner. In spite of the clamor that surrounded the trial, and the heinousness of the offense, the judge could not be swayed to overlook the lack of facts in the case. 1.____

A. avidity
B. meticulousness
C. clemency
D. balance
E. querulousness

2. The pianist played the concerto _______, displaying such facility and skill as has rarely been matched in this old auditorium. 2.____

A. strenuous
B. spiritedly
C. passionately
D. casually
E. deftly

3. The Tanglewood Symphony Orchestra holds its outdoor concerts far from city turmoil in a _______, bucolic setting. 3.____

A. spectacular
B. atavistic
C. serene
D. chaotic
E. catholic

4. Honest satire gives true joy to the thinking man. Thus, the satirist is most _______ when he points out the hypocrisy in human actions. 4.____

A. elated
B. humiliated
C. ungainly
D. repressed
E. disdainful

5. She was a(n) _______ preferred the company of her books to the pleasures of cafe society. 5.____

A. philanthropist
B. stoic
C. exhibitionist
D. extrovert
E. introvert

6. So many people are so convinced that people are driven by _______ motives that they cannot believe that anybody is unselfish! 6.____

A. interior
B. ulterior
C. unworth
D. selfish
E. destructive

7. These _______ results were brought about by a chain of fortuitous events. 7.____

A. unfortunate
B. odd
C. harmful
D. haphazard
E. propitious

8. The bank teller's _______ of the funds was discovered the following month when the auditors examined the books. 8.____

A. embezzlement
B. burglary
C. borrowing
D. assignment
E. theft

9. The monks gathered in the _______ for their evening meal. 9.____

A. lounge
B. auditorium
C. refectory
D. rectory
E. solarium

10. Local officials usually have the responsibility in each area of determining when the need is sufficiently great to _______ withdrawals from the community water supply. 10.____

A. encourage
B. justify
C. discontinue
D. advocate
E. forbid

KEY (CORRECT ANSWERS)

1. D
2. E
3. C
4. A
5. E
6. B
7. D
8. A
9. C
10. B

TEST 4

DIRECTIONS: Each question in this section consists of a sentence in which one word is missing; a blank line indicates where the word has been removed from the sentence. Beneath each sentence are five words, *one* of which is the missing word. You are to select the letter of the missing word by deciding which one of the five words BEST fits in with the meaning of the sentence. *PRINT THE LETTER OF THE CORRECT ANSWER IN THE SPACE AT THE RIGHT*

1. The life of the mining camps as portrayed by Bret Harte–boisterous, material, brawling–was in direct _______ to the contemporary Eastern world of conventional morals and staid deportment depicted by other men of letters. 1.____

   A. model B. parallel C. antithesis
   D. relationship E. response

2. The agreements were to remain in force for three years and were subject to automatic _______ unless terminated by the parties concerned on one month's notice. 2.____

   A. renewal B. abrogation C. amendment
   D. confiscation E. option

3. In a democracy, people are recognized for what they do rather than for their _______. 3.____

   A. alacrity B. ability C. reputation
   D. skill E. pedigree

4. Although he had often loudly proclaimed his _______ concerning world affairs, he actually read widely and was usually the best informed person in his circle. 4.____

   A. weariness B. complacency C. condolence
   D. indifference E. worry

5. This student holds the _______ record of being the sole failure in his class. 5.____

   A. flagrant B. unhappy C. egregious
   D. dubious E. unusual

6. She became enamored _______ acrobat when she witnessed his act. 6.____

   A. of B. with C. for D. by E. about

7. This will _______ all previous wills. 7.____

   A. abrogates B. denies C. supersedes
   D. prevents E. continues

8. In the recent terrible Chicago _______, over ninety children were found dead as a result of the fire. 8.____

   A. hurricane B. destruction C. panic
   D. holocaust E. accident

9. I can ascribe no better reason why he shunned society than that he was a _______. 9.____

   A. mentor B. Centaur C. aristocrat
   D. misanthrope E. failure

10. One who attempts to learn all the known facts before he comes to a conclusion may most aptly be described as a _______. 10.___

A. realist
B. philosopher
C. cynic
D. pessimist
E. skeptic

KEY (CORRECT ANSWERS)

1. C
2. A
3. E
4. D
5. D
6. A
7. C
8. D
9. D
10. E

TEST 5

DIRECTIONS: Each question in this section consists of a sentence in which one word is missing; a blank line indicates where the word has been removed from the sentence. Beneath each sentence are five words, *one* of which is the missing word. You are to select the letter of the missing word by deciding which one of the five words BEST fits in with the meaning of the sentence. *PRINT THE LETTER OF THE CORRECT ANSWER IN THE SPACE AT THE RIGHT.*

1. The prime minister, fleeing from the rebels who had seized the government, sought _______ in the church. 1._____

   A. revenge B. mercy C. relief
   D. salvation E. sanctuary

2. It does not take us long to conclude that it is foolish to fight the _______, and that it is far wiser to accept it. 2._____

   A. inevitable B. inconsequential C. impossible
   D. choice E. invasion

3. _______ is usually defined as an excessively high rate of interest. 3._____

   A. Injustice B. Perjury C. Exorbitant
   D. Embezzlement E. Usury

4. "I ask you, gentlemen of the jury, to find this man guilty since I have _______ the charges brought about him." 4._____

   A. documented B. questioned C. revised
   D. selected E. confused

5. Although the critic was a close friend of the producer, he told him that he could not _______ his play. 5._____

   A. condemn B. prefer C. congratulate
   D. endorse E. revile

6. Knowledge of human nature and motivation is an important _______ in all areas of endeavor. 6._____

   A. object B. incentive C. opportunity
   D. asset E. goal

7. Numbered among the audience were kings, princes, dukes, and even a maharajah, all attempting to _______ another in the glitter of their habiliments and the number of their escorts. 7._____

   A. supersede B. outdo C. guide
   D. vanquish E. equal

8. There seems to be a widespread feeling that peoples who are located below us in respect to latitude are _______ also in respect to intellect and ability. 8._____

   A. superior B. melodramatic C. inferior
   D. ulterior E. contemptible

9. This should be considered a(n) _______ rather than the usual occurrence. 9.___

A. coincidence B. specialty C. development
D. outgrowth E. mirage

10. Those who were considered states' rights adherents in the early part of our history, espoused the diminution of the powers of the national government because they had always been _______ of these powers. 10.___

A. solicitous B. advocates C. apprehensive
D. mindful E. respectful

KEY (CORRECT ANSWERS)

1. E
2. A
3. E
4. A
5. D
6. D
7. B
8. C
9. A
10. C

TEST 6

DIRECTIONS: Each question in this section consists of a sentence in which one word is missing; a blank line indicates where the word has been removed from the sentence. Beneath each sentence are five words, *one* of which is the missing word. You are to select the letter of the missing word by deciding which one of the five words BEST fits in with the meaning of the sentence. *PRINT THE LETTER OF THE CORRECT ANSWER IN THE SPACE AT THE RIGHT.*

1. We can see in retrospect that the high hopes for lasting peace conceived at Versailles in 1919 were _______. 1.____

   A. ingenuous B. transient C. nostalgic
   D. ingenious E. specious

2. One of the constructive effects of Nazism was the passage by the U.N. of a resolution to combat _______. 2.____

   A. armaments B. nationalism C. colonialism
   D. genocide E. geriatrics

3. In our prisons, the role of _______ often gains for certain inmates a powerful position among their fellow prisoners. 3.____

   A. informer B. clerk C. warden D. trusty E. turnkey

4. It is the _______ liar, experienced in the ways of the world, who finally trips upon some incongruous detail. 4.____

   A. consummate B. incorrigible C. congenital
   D. lagrant E. contemptible

5. Anyone who is called a misogynist can hardly be expected to look upon women with _______ contemptuous eyes. 5.____

   A. more than B. nothing less than C. decidedly
   D. other than E. always

6. Demagogues such as Hitler and Mussolini aroused the masses by appealing to their _______ rather than to their intellect. 6.____

   A. emotions B. reason C. nationalism
   D. conquests E. duty

7. He was in great demand as an entertainer for his _______ abilities: he could sing, dance, tell a joke, or relate a story with equally great skill and facility. 7.____

   A. versatile B. logical C. culinary
   D. histrionic E. creative

8. The wise politician is aware that, next to knowing when to seize an opportunity, it is also important to know when to _______ an advantage. 8.____

   A. develop B. seek C. revise
   D. proclaim E. forego

9. Books on psychology inform us that the best way to break a bad habit is to _______ a new habit in its place. 9.____

A. expel
B. substitute
C. conceal
D. curtail
E. supplant

10. The author who uses one word where another uses a whole paragraph, should be considered a _______ writer. 10.____

A. successful
B. grandiloquent
C. experienced
D. prolix
E. succinct

KEY (CORRECT ANSWERS)

1.	A	6.	A
2.	D	7.	A
3.	A	8.	E
4.	A	9.	B
5.	D	10.	E

SENTENCE COMPLETION

EXAMINATION SECTION

TEST 1

DIRECTIONS: Each question in this part consists of a sentence in which one word is missing; a blank line indicates where the word has been removed from the sentence. Beneath each sentence are five words, one of which is the missing word. You are to select the number of the missing word by deciding which one of the five words BEST fits in with the meaning of the sentence. *PRINT THE LETTER OF THE CORRECT ANSWER IN THE SPACE AT THE RIGHT.*

1. Although they had little interest in the game they were playing, rather than be _______, they played it through to the end. 1.____

   A. inactive B. inimical C. busy
   D. complacent E. vapid

2. That he was unworried and at peace with the world could be, perhaps, observed from his _______ brow. 2.____

   A. unwrinkled B. wrinkled C. furrowed
   D. twisted E. askew

3. Among the hundreds of workers in the assembly plant of the factory, one was _______ because of his skill and speed. 3.____

   A. steadfast B. condemned C. consistent
   D. outstanding E. eager

4. The story of the invention of many of our best known machines is a consistent one: they are the result of a long series of experiments by many people; thus, the Wright Brothers in 1903 _______ the airplane rather than invented it. 4.____

   A. popularized B. regulated C. perfected
   D. contrived E. developed

5. As soon as the former political exile returned to his native country, he looked up old supporters, particularly those whom he knew to be _______ and whose help he might need. 5.____

   A. potent B. pusillanimous C. attentive
   D. free E. retired

6. A recent study of the New Deal shows that no other man than the President could have brought together so many _______ interests and combined them into so effective a political organization. 6.____

   A. secret B. interior C. predatory
   D. harmonious E. conflicting

7. A study of tides presents an interesting _______ in that, while the forces that set them in motion are universal in application, presumably affecting all parts of our world without distinction, the action of tides in particular areas is completely local in nature. 7.____

   A. phenomenon B. maneuver C. paradox
   D. quality E. spontaneity

8. Many of the facts that are found in the ancient archives constitute _______ that help shed light upon human activities in the past. 8.____

A. facts
B. reminders
C. particles
D. sources
E. indications

9. It is a regrettable fact that in a caste society which deems manual toil a mark of _______, rarely does the laborer improve his social position or gain political power. 9.____

A. inferiority
B. consolation
C. fortitude
D. hardship
E. brilliance

10. As a generalization, one can correctly say that crises in history are caused by the re-opening of questions which have been safely _______ for long periods of time. 10.____

A. debated
B. joined
C. recondite
D. settled
E. unanswered

KEY (CORRECT ANSWERS)

1. A
2. A
3. D
4. C
5. A

6. E
7. C
8. D
9. A
10. A

TEST 2

DIRECTIONS: Each question in this part consists of a sentence in which one word is missing; a blank line indicates where the word has been removed from the sentence. Beneath each sentence are five words, one of which is the missing word. You are to select the number of the missing word by deciding which one of the five words BEST fits in with the meaning of the sentence. *PRINT THE LETTER OF THE CORRECT ANSWER IN THE SPACE AT THE RIGHT.*

1. We can see in retrospect that the high hopes for lasting peace conceived at Versailles in 1919 were _______. 1.____

   A. ingenuous B. transient C. nostalgic
   D. ingenious E. species

2. One of the constructive effects of Nazism was the passage by the U.N. of a resolution to combat _______. 2.____

   A. armaments B. nationalism C. colonialism
   D. genocide E. geriatrics

3. In our prisons, the role of _______ often gains for certain inmates a powerful position among their fellow prisoners. 3.____

   A. informer B. clerk C. warden
   D. trusty E. turnkey

4. It is the _______ liar, experienced in the ways of the world, who finally trips upon some incongruous detail. 4.____

   A. consummate B. incorrigible C. congenital
   D. flagrant E. contemptible

5. Anyone who is called a misogynist can hardly be expected to look upon women with _______ contemptuous eyes. 5.____

   A. more than B. nothing less than C. decidedly
   D. other than E. always

6. Demagogues such as Hitler and Mussolini aroused the masses by appealing to their _______ rather than to their intellect. 6.____

   A. emotions B. reason C. nationalism
   D. conquests E. duty

7. He was in great demand as an entertainer for his _______ abilities: he could sing, dance, tell a joke, or relate a story with equally great skill and facility. 7.____

   A. versatile B. logical C. culinary
   D. histrionic E. creative

8. The wise politician is aware that, next to knowing when to seize an opportunity, it is also important to know when to _______ an advantage. 8.____

   A. develop B. seek C. revise D. proclaim E. forego

9. Books on psychology inform us that the best way to break a bad habit is to ______ a new habit in its place. 9.___

A. expel
B. substitute
C. conceal
D. curtail
E. supplant

10. The author who uses one word where another uses a whole paragraph, should be considered a ______ writer. 10.___

A. successful
B. grandiloquent
C. succinct
D. prolix
E. experienced

KEYS (CORRECT ANSWERS)

1. A
2. D
3. A
4. A
5. D

6. A
7. A
8. E
9. B
10. C

TEST 3

DIRECTIONS: Each question in this part consists of a sentence in which one word is missing; a blank line indicates where the word has been removed from the sentence. Beneath each sentence are five words, one of which is the missing word. You are to select the number of the missing word by deciding which one of the five words BEST fits in with the meaning of the sentence. *PRINT THE LETTER OF THE CORRECT ANSWER IN THE SPACE AT THE RIGHT.*

1. The prime minister, fleeing from the rebels who had seized the government, sought _______ in the church. 1._____

   A. revenge B. mercy C. relief
   D. salvation E. sanctuary

2. It does not take us long to conclude that it is foolish to fight the _______, and that it is far wiser to accept it. 2._____

   A. inevitable B. inconsequential C. impossible
   D. choice E. invasion

3. _______ is usually defined as an excessively high rate of interest. 3._____

   A. Injustice B. Perjury C. Exorbitant
   D. Embezzlement E. Usury

4. "I ask you, gentlemen of the jury, to find this man guilty since I have _______ the charges brought against him." 4._____

   A. documented B. questioned C. revised
   D. selected E. confused

5. Although the critic was a close friend of the producer, he told him that he could not _______ his play. 5._____

   A. condemn B. prefer C. congratulate
   D. endorse E. revile

6. Knowledge of human nature and motivation is an important _______ in all areas of endeavor. 6._____

   A. object B. incentive C. opportunity
   D. asset E. goal

7. Numbered among the audience were kings, princes, dukes, and even a maharajah, all attempting to _______ one another in the glitter of their habiliments and the number of their escorts. 7._____

   A. supersede B. outdo C. guide
   D. vanquish E. equal

8. There seems to be a widespread feeling that peoples who are located below us in respect to latitude are _______ also in respect to intellect and ability. 8._____

   A. superior B. melodramatic C. inferior
   D. ulterior E. contemptible

9. This should be considered a(n) ______ rather than the usual occurrence. 9.___

   A. coincidence B. specialty C. development
   D. outgrowth E. mirage

10. Those who were considered states' rights aherents in the early part of our history espoused the diminution of the powers of the national government because they had always been ______ of these powers. 10.___

   A. solicitous B. advocates C. apprehensive
   D. mindful E. respectful

KEYS (CORRECT ANSWERS)

1. E
2. A
3. E
4. A
5. D

6. D
7. B
8. C
9. A
10. C

TEST 4

DIRECTIONS: Each question in this part consists of a sentence in which one word is missing; a blank line indicates where the word has been removed from the sentence. Beneath each sentence are five words, one of which is the missing word. You are to select the number of the missing word by deciding which one of the five words BEST fits in with the meaning of the sentence. *PRINT THE LETTER OF THE CORRECT ANSWER IN THE SPACE AT THE RIGHT.*

1. The life of the mining camps as portrayed by Bret Harte - boisterous, material, brawling - was in direct _______ to the contemporary Eastern world of conventional morals and staid deportment depicted by other men of letters. 1._____

   A. model B. parallel C. antithesis
   D. relationship E. response

2. The agreements were to remain in force for three years and were subject to automatic _______ unless terminated by the parties concerned on one month's notice. 2._____

   A. renewal B. abrogation C. amendment
   D. confiscation E. option

3. In a democracy, people are recognized for what they do rather than for their _______. 3._____

   A. alacrity B. ability C. reputation
   D. skill E. pedigree

4. Although he had often loudly proclaimed his _______ concerning world affairs, he actually read widely and was usually the best informed person in his circle. 4._____

   A. weariness B. complacency C. condolence
   D. indifference E. worry

5. This student holds the _______ record of being the sole failure in his class. 5._____

   A. flagrant B. unhappy C. egregious
   D. dubious E. unusual

6. She became enamored _______ the acrobat when she witnessed his act. 6._____

   A. of B. with C. for D. by E. about

7. This will _______ all previous wills. 7._____

   A. abrogates B. denies C. supersedes
   D. prevents E. continues

8. In the recent terrible Chicago _______, over ninety children were found dead as a result of the fire. 8._____

   A. hurricane B. destruction C. panic
   D. holocaust E. accident

9. I can ascribe no better reason why he shunned society than that he was a _______. 9._____

   A. mentor B. Centaur C. aristocrat
   D. misanthrope E. failure

10. One who attempts to learn all the known facts before he comes to a conclusion may most aptly be described as a 10.____

A. realist
B. philosopher
C. cynic
D. pessimist
E. skeptic

KEY (CORRECT ANSWERS)

1. C
2. A
3. E
4. D
5. D
6. A
7. C
8. D
9. D
10. E

TEST 5

DIRECTIONS: Each question in this part consists of a sentence in which one word is missing; a blank line indicates where the word has been removed from the sentence. Beneath each sentence are five words, one of which is the missing word. You are to select the number of the missing word by deciding which one of the five words BEST fits in with the meaning of the sentence. *PRINT THE LETTER OF THE CORRECT ANSWER IN THE SPACE AT THE RIGHT.*

1. The judge exercised commendable _______ in dismissing the charge against the prisoner. In spite of the clamor that surrounded the trial, and the heinousness of the offense, the judge could not be swayed to overlook the lack of facts in the case. 1.____

   A. avidity B. meticulousness C. clemency
   D. balance E. querulousness

2. The pianist played the concerto _______, displaying such facility and skill as has rarely been matched in this old auditorium. 2.____

   A. strenuously B. deftly C. passionately
   D. casually E. spiritedly

3. The Tanglewood Symphony Orchestra holds its outdoor concerts far from city turmoil in a _______, bucolic setting. 3.____

   A. spectacular B. atavistic C. serene
   D. chaotic E. catholic

4. Honest satire gives true joy to the thinking man. Thus, the satirist is most _______ when he points out the hypocrisy in human actions. 4.____

   A. elated B. humiliated C. ungainly
   D. repressed E. disdainful

5. She was a(n) _______ who preferred the company of her books to the pleasures of cafe society. 5.____

   A. philanthropist B. stoic C. exhibitionist
   D. extrovert E. introvert

6. So many people are so convinced that people are driven by _______ motives that they cannot believe that anybody is unselfish! 6.____

   A. interior B. ulterior C. unworthy
   D. selfish E. destructive

7. These _______ results were brought about by a chain of fortuitous events. 7.____

   A. unfortunate B. odd C. harmful
   D. haphazard E. propitious

8. The bank teller's _______ of the funds was discovered the following month when the auditors examined the books. 8.____

   A. embezzlement B. burglary C. borrowing
   D. assignment E. theft

9. The monks gathered in the _______ for their evening meal. 9.___

A. lounge B. auditorium C. refectory
D. rectory E. solarium

10. Local officials usually have the responsibility in each area of determining when the need is sufficiently great to _______ withdrawals from the community water supply. 10.___

A. encourage B. justify C. discontinue
D. advocate E. forbid

KEY (CORRECT ANSWERS)

1. D
2. B
3. C
4. A
5. E

6. B
7. D
8. A
9. C
10. B

READING COMPREHENSION
UNDERSTANDING AND INTERPRETING WRITTEN MATERIAL

EXAMINATION SECTION
TEST 1

Questions 1-40.

DIRECTIONS: Read the following passages, and select the most appropriate word from the five alternatives provided for each deleted word. Print the letter of the correct answer in the space at the right.

PASSAGE I

Bridges are built to allow a continuous flow of highway and railway traffic across water lying in their paths. But engineers cannot forget the fact that river traffic, too, is essential to our economy. The role of 1 is important. To keep these vessels moving freely, bridges are built high enough, when possible, to let them pass underneath. Sometimes, however, channels must accommodate very tall ships. It may be uneconomical to build a tall enough bridge. The 2 would be too high. To save money, engineers build movable bridges.

1. A. wind B. boats C. weight D. wires E. experience 1.____

2. A. levels B. cost C. standards D. waves E. deck 2.____

In the swing bridge, the middle part pivots or swings open. When the bridge is closed, this section joins the two ends of the bridge, blocking tall vessels. But this section 3. When swung open, it is perpendicular to the ends of the bridge, creating two free channels for river traffic. With swing bridges, channel width is limited by the bridge's piers. The largest swing bridge provides only a 75-meter channel. Such channels are sometimes too 4. In such cases, a bascule bridge may be built.

3. A. stands B. floods C. wears D. turns E. supports 3.____

4. A. narrow B. rough C. long D. deep E. straight 4.____

Bascule bridges are drawbridges with two arms that swing upward. They provide an opening as wide as the span. They are also versatile. These bridges are not limited to being fully opened or fully closed. They can be 5 in many ways. They can be fixed at different angles to accommodate different vessels.

5. A. approached B. crossed C. lighted D. planned E. positioned 5.____

In vertical lift bridges, the center remains horizontal. Towers at both ends allow the center to be lifted like an elevator. One interesting variation of this kind of bridge was built during World War II. A lift bridge was desired, but there were wartime shortages of the steel and machinery needed for the towers. It was hard to find enough 6. An ingenious engineer designed the bridge so that it did not have to be raised above traffic. Instead it was 7. It could be submerged seven meters below the river surface. Ships sailed over it.

6. A. work B. material C. time D. power E. space 6.___

7. A. burned B. emptied C. secured D. shared E. lowered 7.___

PASSAGE II

Before anesthetics were discovered, surgery was carried out under very severe time restrictions. Patients were awake, tossing and screaming in terrible pain. Surgeons were forced to hurry in order to constrain suffering and minimize shock. 8 was essential. Haste, however, did not make for good outcomes in surgery. No surprise, then, that the 9 were often poor.

8. A. Blood B. Silence C. Speed D. Water E. Money 8.___

9. A. quarters B. teeth C. results D. materials E. families 9.___

The discovery of anesthetics happened, in part, by accident. During the early 1800' s, nitrous oxide and ether were used for entertainment. At "ether frolics" in theaters, volunteers would breathe these gases, become lightheaded, and run around the stage laughing and dancing. By chance, a Connecticut dentist saw such a 10. One volunteer banged his leg against a sharp edge. But he did not 11. He paid no attention to his wound, as though he felt nothing. This gave the dentist the idea of using gas to kill pain.

10. A. show B. machine C. face D. source E. growth 10.___

11. A. dream B. recover C. succeed D. agree E. notice 11.___

At first, using the "open drip method," ether and chloroform were filtered through a cotton pad placed over the mouth and nose. This direct dose was difficult to regulate and irritating to the nose and throat. Patients would hold their breath, cough, or gag. This made it impossible for them to relax, let alone sleep. Consequently, surgery was often 12. It couldn't begin until the patient had quieted and the anesthesia had taken hold.

12. A. delayed B. required C. blamed D. observed E. repeated 12.___

Today's procedures are safer and more accurate. In the "closed method," a fixed amount of gas is released from sealed bottles into an inhalator bag when the patient exhales. He inhales this gas through tubes with his next breath. In this way, the gas is 13. The system carefully regulates how much gas reaches the patient.

13. A. heated B. controlled C. cleaned D. selected E. wasted 13.___

For dentistry and minor operations, patients need not be asleep. Newer anesthetics can be used which deaden nerves only in the affected part of the body. These 14 anesthetics offer several advantages. For instance, since the anesthesia is fairly light and patients remain awake, they can cooperate with their doctors.

14. A. local B. natural C. ancient D. heavy E. thyee 14.____

PASSAGE III

An indispensable element in the development of telephony was the continual improvement of telephone station instruments, those operating units located at the client's premises. Modern units normally consist of a transmitter, receiver, and transformer. They also contain a bell or equivalent summoning device, a mechanism for controlling the unit's connection to the client's line, and various associated items, like dials. All of these 15 have changed over the years. The transmitter, especially, has undergone enormous refinement during the last century.

15. A. parts B. costs C. services D. models E. routes 15.____

Bell's original electromagnetic transmitter functioned likewise as receiver, the same instrument being held alternately to mouth and ear. But having to 16 the instrument this; way was inconvenient. Suggestions understandably emerged for mounting the transmitter and receiver onto a common handle, thereby creating what are now known as handsets. Transmitter and receiver were, in; fact, later 17 his way. Combination handsets were produced for commercial utilization late in the nineteenth century, but prospects for their acceptance were uncertain as the initial quality of transmissions with the handsets was disappointing. But 18 transmissions followed. With adequately high transmission standards attained, acceptance of handsets was virtually assured.

16. A. store B. use C. test D. strip E. clean 16.____

17. A. grounded B. marked C. covered D. priced E. coupled 17.____

18. A. shorter B. fewer C. better D. faster E. cheaper 18.____

Among the most significant improvements in transmitters has been the enormous amplification (up to a thousandfold) of speech sounds. This increased 19 has benefited tele-communicat ions enormously. Nineteenth century telephone conversations frequently were only marginally audible, whereas nowadays even murmured conversations can be transmitted successfully, barring unusual atmospheric or electronic disturbances.

19. A. distance B. speed C. market D. volume E. number 19.____

Vocal quality over nineteenth century instruments was distorted, the speaker not readily identifiable. By comparison, current sound is characterized by considerably greater naturalism. Modern telephony produces speech sounds more nearly resembling an individual's actual voice. Thus it is easier to 20 the speaker. A considerable portion of this improvement is attributable to practical applications of laboratory investigations concerning the mechanisms of human speech and audition. These 21 have exerted a profound influence. Their results prompted technical innovations in modern transmitter design which contributed appreciably to the excellent communication available nowadays.

20. A. time B. help C. bill 20.___
D. stop E. recognize

21. A. studies B. rates C. materials 21.___
D. machines E. companies

PASSAGE IV

The dramatic events of December 7, 1941, plunged this nation into war. The full 22 of the war we can not even now comprehend, but one of the effects stands out in sharp relief -- the coming of the air age. The airplane, which played a relatively 23 part in World War I, has already soared to heights undreamed of save by the few with mighty vision.

In wartime the airplane is the 24 on wings and the battleship that flies. To man in his need it symbolizes deadly, extremes; friend or foe; deliverance or 25.

It is a powerful instrument of war revolutionizing military strategy, but its peacetime role is just as 26. This new master of time and space, fruit of man's inventive genius, has come to stay, smalling the earth and smoothing its surface.

To all of us, then, to youth, and to 27 alike. comes the winged challenge to get ourselves ready--to 28 ourselves for living in an age which the airplane seems destined to mold.

22. A. destruction B. character C. history 22.___
D. import E. picture

23. A. important B. dull C. vast D. unknown E. minor 23.___

24. A. giant B. ant C. monster D. artillery E. robot 24.___

25. A. ecstasy B. bombardment C. death 25.___
D. denial E. survival

26. A. revolting B. revolutionary C. residual 26.___
D. reliable E. regressive

27. A. animals B. nations C. women D. men E. adult 27.___

28. A. distract B. engage C. determine D. deter E. orient 28.___

PASSAGE V

Let us consider how voice training may contribute to 29 development and an improved social 30.

In the first place, it has been fairly well established that individuals tend to become what they believe 31 people think them to be.

When people react more favorably toward us because our voices 32 the impression that we are friendly, competent, and interesting, there is a strong tendency for us to develop those 33 in our personality.

If we are treated with respect by others, we soon come to have more respect for 34.

Then, too, one's own consciousness of having a pleasant, effective voice of which he does not need to be ashamed contributes materially to a feeling of poise, self-confidence, and a just pride in himself.

A good voice, like good clothes, can do much for an 35 that otherwise might be inclined to droop.

29. A. facial B. material C. community 29.___
D. personality E. physical

30. A. adjustment B. upheaval C. development 30.____
D. bias E. theories

31. A. some B. hostile C. jealous D. inferior E. other 31.____

32. A. betray B. imply C. destroy 32.____
D. transfigure E. convey

33. A. defects B. qualities C. techniques 33.____
D. idiosyncrasies E. quirks

34. A. others B. their children C. their teachers 34.____
D. ourselves E. each other

35. A. mind B. heart C. brain D. feeling E. ego. 35.____

PASSAGE VI

How are symphony orchestras launched, kept boing, and built up in smaller communities? Recent reports from five of them suggest that, though the 36 changes, certain elements are fairly common. One thing shines out; 37 is essential.

Also, aside from the indispensable, instrumentalists who play, the following personalities, either singly, or preferably in 38. seem to be the chief needs; a conductor who wants to conduct so badly he will organize his own orchestra if it is the only way he can get one; a manager with plenty of resourcefulness in rounding up audiences and finding financial support; an energetic community leader, generally a woman, who will take up locating the orchestra as a 39; and generous visiting soloists who will help draw those who are 40 that anything local can be used.

36. A. world B. pattern C. reason D. scene E. cast 36.____

37. A. hatred B. love C. enthusiasm 37.____
D. participation E. criticism

38. A. combination B. particular C. isolation 38.____
D. sympathy E. solitary

39. A. chore B. duty C. hobby D. delight E. career 39.____

40. A. convinced B. skeptical C. happy 40.____
D. unhappy E. unsure

KEY (CORRECT ANSWERS)

1.	B	11.	E	21.	A	31.	E
2.	B	12.	A	22.	D	32.	E
3.	D	13.	B	23.	E	33.	B
4.	A	14.	A	24.	D	34.	D
5.	E	15.	A	25.	C	35.	E
6.	B	16.	B	26.	B	36.	B
7.	E	17.	E	27.	E	37.	C
8.	C	18.	C	28.	E	38.	A
9.	C	19.	D	29.	D	39.	C
10.	A	20.	E	30.	A	40.	B

READING COMPREHENSION
UNDERSTANDING AND INTERPRETING WRITTEN MATERIAL

EXAMINATION SECTION

DIRECTIONS: Each question or incomplete statement is followed by several suggested answers or completions. Select the one that BEST answers the question or completes the statement. *PRINT THE LETTER OF THE CORRECT ANSWER IN THE SPACE AT THE RIGHT.*

TEST 1

Skiing has recently become one of the more popular sports in the United States. Because of its popularity, thousands of winter vacationers are flying north rather than south. In many areas, reservations are required months ahead of time.

I discovered the accommodation shortage through an unfortunate experience. On a sunny Saturday morning, I set out from Denver for the beckoning slopes of Aspen, Colorado. After passing signs for other ski areas, I finally reached my destination. Naturally, I lost no time in heading for the nearest tow. After a stimulating afternoon of miscalculated stem turns, I was famished. Well, one thing led to another, and it must have been eight o'clock before I concerned myself with a bed for my bruised and aching bones.

It took precisely one phone call to ascertain the lack of lodgings in the Aspen area. I had but one recourse. My auto and I started the treacherous jaunt over the pass and back towards Denver. Along the way, I went begging for a bed. Finally, a jolly tavernkeeper took pity, and for only thirty dollars a night allowed me the privilege of staying in a musty, dirty, bathless room above his tavern.

1. The author's problem would have been avoided if he had 1.____

   A. not tired himself out skiing
   B. taken a bus instead of driving
   C. looked for food as soon as he arrived
   D. arranged for accommodations well ahead of his trip
   E. answer cannot be determined from the information given

TEST 2

Helen Keller was born in 1880 in Tuscumbia, Alabama. When she was two years old, she lost her sight and hearing as the result of an illness. In 1886, she became the pupil of Anne Sullivan, who taught Helen to *see* with her fingertips, to *hear* with her feet and hands, and to communicate with other people. Miss Sullivan succeeded in arousing Helen's curiosity and interest by spelling the names of objects into her hand. At the end of three years, Helen had mastered the manual and the braille alphabet and could read and write.

2. When did Helen Keller lose her sight and hearing? 2.____

TEST 3

Sammy got to school ten minutes after the school bell had rung. He was breathing hard and had a black eye. His face was dirty and scratched. One leg of his pants was torn.

Tommy was late to school, too; however, he was only five minutes late. Like Sammy, he was breathing hard, but he was happy and smiling.

3. Sammy and Tommy had been fighting. Who probably won? 3.___

   A. Sammy
   B. Tommy
   C. Cannot tell from story
   D. The teacher
   E. The school

TEST 4

This is like a game to see if you can tell what the nonsense word in the paragraph stands for. The nonsense word is just a silly word for something that you know very well. Read the paragraph and see if you can tell what the underlined nonsense word stands for.

You can wash your hands and face in zup. You can even take a bath in it. When people swim, they are in the zup. Everyone drinks zup.

4. Zup is PROBABLY 4.___

   A. milk B. pop C. soap D. water E. soup

TEST 5

After two weeks of unusually high-speed travel, we reached Xeno, a small planet whose population, though never before visited by Earthmen, was listed as *friendly* in the INTERSTELLAR GAZETTEER.

On stepping lightly (after all, the gravity of Xeno is scarcely more than twice that of our own moon) from our spacecraft, we saw that *friendly* was an understatement. We were immediately surrounded by Frangibles of various colors, mostly pinkish or orange, who held out their *hands* to us. Imagine our surprise when their *hands* actually merged with ours as we tried to shake them!

Then, before we could stop them (how could we have stopped them?), two particularly pink Frangibles simply stepped right into two eminent scientists among our party, who immediately lit up with the same pink glow. While occupied in this way, the scientists reported afterwards they suddenly discovered they *knew* a great deal about Frangibles and life on Xeno.

Apparently, Frangibles could take themselves apart atomically and enter right into any other substance. They communicated by thought waves, occasionally merging *heads* for greater clarity. Two Frangibles who were in love with each other would spend most of their time merged into one; they were a bluish-green color unless they were having a lover's quarrel, when they turned gray.

5. In order to find out about an object which interested him, what would a Frangible MOST likely do? 5.____

A. Take it apart
B. Enter into it
C. Study it scientifically
D. Ask earth scientists about it
E. Wait to see if it would change color

TEST 6

This is like a game to see if you can tell what the nonsense word in the paragraph stands for. The nonsense word is just a silly word for something that you know very well. Read the paragraph and see if you can tell what the underlined nonsense word stands for.

Have you ever smelled a <u>mart</u>? They smell very good. Bees like <u>marts</u>. They come in many colors. <u>Marts</u> grow in the earth, and they usually bloom in the spring.

6. <u>Marts</u> are PROBABLY 6.____

A. bugs B. flowers C. perfume
D. pies E. cherries

TEST 7

Christmas was only a few days away. The wind was strong and cold. The walks were covered with snow. The downtown streets were crowded with people. Their faces were hidden by many packages as they went in one store after another. They all tried to move faster as they looked at the clock.

7. When did the story PROBABLY happen? 7.____

A. November 28 B. December 1 C. December 21
D. December 25 E. December 28

TEST 8

THE WAYFARER

The wayfarer,
Perceiving the pathway to truth,
Was struck with astonishment.
It was thickly grown with weeds.
Ha, he said,
I see that no one has passed here
In a long time.
Later he saw that each weed
Was a singular knife,
Well, he mumbled at last,
Doubtless there are other roads.

8. *I see that no one has passed here In a long time.* 8.__
What do the above lines from the poem mean?

A. The way of truth is popular.
B. People are fascinated by the truth.
C. Truth comes and goes like the wind.
D. The truth is difficult to recognize.
E. Few people are searching for the truth.

TEST 9

Any attempt to label an entire generation is unrewarding, and yet the generation which went through the last war, or at least could get a drink easily once it was over, seems to possess a uniform, general quality which demands an adjective. It was John Kerouac, the author of a fine, neglected novel, THE TOWN AND THE CITY, who finally came up with it. It was several years ago, when the face was harder to recognize, but he had a sharp, sympathetic eye, and one day he said, *You know, this is really a beat generation.* The origins of the word *beat* are obscure, but the meaning is only too clear to most Americans. More than mere weariness, it implies the feeling of having been used, of being raw. It involves a sort of nakedness of mind, and, ultimately, of soul; a feeling of being reduced to the bedrock of consciousness. In short, it means being undramatically pushed up against the wall of oneself. A man is beat whenever he goes for broke and waters the sum of his resources on a single number; and the young generation has done that continually from early youth.

9. What does the writer suggest when he mentions a *fine, neglected novel*? 9.__

A. Kerouac had the right idea about the war
B. Kerouac had a clear understanding of the new post-war generation
C. Kerouac had not received the recognition of THE TOWN AND THE CITY that was deserved
D. Kerouac had the wrong idea about the war.
E. All of the above

TEST 10

One spring, Farmer Brown had an unusually good field of wheat. Whenever he saw any birds in this field, he got his gun and shot as many of them as he could. In the middle of the summer, he found that his wheat was being ruined by insects. With no birds to feed on them, the insects had multiplied very fast. What Farmer Brown did not understand was this: A bird is not simply an animal that eats food the farmer may want for himself. Instead, it is one of many links in the complex surroundings, or environment, in which we live.

How much grain a farmer can raise on an acre of ground depends on many factors. All of these factors can be divided into two big groups. Such things as the richness of the soil, the amount of rainfall, the amount of sunlight, and the temperature belong together in one of these groups. This group may be called <u>nonliving factors</u>. The second group may be called <u>living factors</u>. The living factors in any plant's environment are animals and other plants. Wheat, for example, may be damaged by wheat rust, a tiny plant that feeds on wheat, or it may be eaten by plant-eating animals such as birds or grasshoppers...

It is easy to see that the relations of plants and animals to their environment are very complex, and that any change in the environment is likely to bring about a whole series of changes.

10. What does the passage suggest a good farmer should understand about nature? 10.____

A. Insects are harmful to plants
B. Birds are not harmful to plants
C. Wheat may be damaged by both animals and other plants
D. The amount of wheat he can raise depends on two factors: birds and insects
E. A change in one factor of plants' surroundings may cause other factors to change

11. What important idea about nature does the writer want us to understand? 11.____

A. Farmer Brown was worried about the heavy rainfall
B. Nobody needs to have such destructive birds around
C. Farmer Brown did not want the temperature to change
D. All insects need not only wheat rust but grasshoppers
E. All living things are dependent on other living things

TEST 11

For a 12-year-old, I've been around a lot because my father's in the Army. I have been to New York and to Paris. When I was nine, my parents took me to Rome. I didn't like Europe very much because the people don't speak the same language I do. When I am older, my mother says I can travel by myself. I think I will like that. Ever since I was 13, I have wanted to go to Canada.

12. Why can't everything this person said be TRUE? 12.____

A. 12-year-olds can't travel alone
B. No one can travel that much in 12 years
C. There is a conflict in the ages used in the passage
D. 9-year-olds can't travel alone
E. He is a liar

TEST 12

Between April and October, the Persian Gulf is dotted with the small boats of pearl divers. Some seventy-five thousand of them are busy diving down and bringing up pearl-bearing oysters. These oysters are not the kind we eat. The edible oyster produces pearls of little or no value. You may have heard tales of divers who discovered pearls and sold them for great sums of money. These stories are entertaining but not accurate.

13. The Persian Gulf has many 13._

    A. large boats of pearl divers
    B. pearl divers who eat oysters
    C. edible oysters that produce pearls
    D. non-edible oysters that produce pearls
    E. edible oysters that do not produce pearls

TEST 13

Art says that the polar ice cap is melting at the rate of 3% per year. Bert says that this isn't true because the polar ice cap is really melting at the rate of 7% per year.

14. We know for certain that 14._

    A. Art is wrong
    B. Bert is wrong
    C. they are both wrong
    D. they both might be right
    E. they can't both be right

TEST 14

FORTUNE AND MEN'S EYES

Shakespeare

1. When, in disgrace with fortune and men's eyes,
2. I all alone beweep my outcast state,
3. And trouble deaf heaven with my bootless cries,
4. And look upon myself and curse my fate,
5. Wishing me like to one more rich in hope,
6. Featured like him, like him with friends possessed
7. Desiring this man's art, and that man's scope,
8. With what I most enjoy contented least;
9. Yet in these thoughts myself almost despising,
10. Haply I think on thee; and then my state,
11. Like to the lark at break of day arising
12. From sullen earth, sings hymns at heaven's gate;
13. For thy sweet love remembered, such wealth brings
14. That then I scorn to change my state with kings.

15. What saves this man from wishing to be different than he is? 15.____

    A. Such wealth brings
    B. Hymns at heaven's gate
    C. The lark at break of day
    D. Thy sweet love remembered
    E. Change my state with kings

TEST 15

My name is Gregory Gotrocks, and I live in Peoria, Illinois. I sell tractors. In June 1952, the Gotrocks Tractor Company (my dad happens to be the president) sent me to Nepal-Tibet to check on our sales office there.

Business was slow, and I had a lot of time to kill. I decided to see Mt. Everest so that I could tell everyone back in Peoria that I had seen it.

It was beautiful; I was spellbound. I simply had to see what the view looked like from the top. So I started up the northwest slope. Everyone know that this is the best route to take. It took me three long hours to reach the top, but the climb was well worth it.

16. Gregory Gotrocks went to see Mt. Everest so that he could 16.____

    A. see some friends
    B. sell some tractors
    C. take a picture of it
    D. plant a flag at its base
    E. entertain his friends back home

TEST 16

Suburbanites are not irresponsible. Indeed, what is striking about the young couples' march along the abyss is the earnestness and precision with which they go about it. They are extremely budget-conscious. They can rattle off most of their monthly payments down to the last penny; one might say that even their impulse buying is deliberately planned. They are conscientious in meeting obligations and rarely do they fall delinquent in their accounts.

They are exponents of what could be called budgetism. This does not mean that they actually keep formal budgets – quite the contrary. The beauty of budgetism is that one doesn't have to keep a budget at all. It's done automatically. In the new middle-class rhythms of life, obligations are homogenized, for the overriding aim is to have oneself precommitted to regular, unvarying monthly payments on all the major items.

Americans used to be divided into three sizable groups: those who thought of money obligations in terms of the week, of the month, and of the year. Many people remain at both ends of the scale; but with the widening of the middle class, the mortgage payments are firmly geared to a thirty-day cycle, and any dissonant peaks and valleys are anathema. Just as young couples are now paying winter fuel bills in equal monthly fractions through the year, so they seek to spread out all the other heavy seasonal obligations they can anticipate. If vendors will not oblige by accepting equal monthly installments, the purchasers will smooth out the load themselves by floating loans.

It is, suburbanites cheerfully explain, a matter of psychology. They don't trust themselves. In self-entrapment is security. They try to budget so tightly that there is no unappropriated funds, for they know these would burn a hole in their pocket. Not merely out of greed for goods, then, do they commit themselves; it is protection they want, too. And though it would be extreme to say that they go into debt to be secure, carefully chartered debt does give them a certain peace of mind – and in suburbia this is more coveted than luxury itself.

17. What is the *abyss* along which the young couples are marching? 17._

    A. Nuclear war
    B. Unemployment
    C. Mental breakdown
    D. Financial disaster
    E. Catastrophic illness

18. What conclusion does the author reach concerning carefully chartered debt among young couples in the United States today? 18._
    It

    A. is a symbol of love
    B. brings marital happiness
    C. helps them to feel secure
    D. enables them to acquire wealth
    E. provides them with material goods

TEST 17

Read the verse and fill in the space beside the object described in the verse.

You see me when I'm right or wrong;
My face I never hide.
My hands move slowly round and round
And o'er me minutes glide.

19. A. ___ Book B. ___ Clock C. ___ Record 19.____
D. ___ Table E. ___ Lock

TEST 18

Until about thirty years ago, the village of Nayon seems to have been a self-sufficient agricultural community with a mixture of native and sixteenth century Spanish customs. Lands were abandoned when too badly eroded. The balance between population and resources allowed a minimum subsistence. A few traders exchanged goods between Quito and the villages in the tropical barrancas, all within a radius of ten miles. Houses had dirt floors, thatched roofs, and pole walls that were sometimes plastered with mud. Guinea pigs ran freely about each house and were the main meat source. Most of the population spoke no Spanish. Men wore long hair and concerned themselves chiefly with farming.

The completion of the Guayaquil-Quito railway in 1908 brought the first real contacts with industrial civilization to the high inter-Andean valley. From this event gradually flowed not only technological changes but new ideas and social institutions. Feudal social relationships no longer seemed right and immutable; medicine and public health improved; elementary education became more common; urban Quito began to expand; and finally, and perhaps least important so far, modern industries began to appear, although even now on a most modest scale.

In 1948-49, the date of our visit, only two men wore their hair long; and only two old-style houses remained. If guinea pigs were kept, they were penned; their flesh was now a luxury food, and beef the most common meat. Houses were of adobe or fired brick, usually with tile roofs, and often contained five or six rooms, some of which had plank or brick floors. Most of the population spoke Spanish. There was no resident priest, but an appointed government official and a policeman represented authority. A six-teacher school provided education. Clothing was becoming citified; for men it often included overalls for work and a tailored suit, white shirt, necktie, and felt hat for trips to Quito. Attendance at church was low, and many festivals had been abandoned. Volleyball or soccer was played weekly in the plaza by young men who sometimes wore shorts, blazers, and berets. There were few shops, for most purchases were made in Quito, and from there came most of the food, so that there was a far more varied diet than twenty-five years ago. There were piped water and sporadic health services; in addition, most families patronized Quito doctors in emergencies.

The crops and their uses had undergone change. Maize, or Indian corn, was still the primary crop, but very little was harvested as grain. Almost all was sold in Quito as green corn to eat boiled on the cob, and a considerable amount of the corn eaten as grain in Nayon was imported. Beans, which do poorly here, were grown on a small scale for household consumption. Though some squash was eaten, most was exported. Sweet potatoes, tomatoes, cabbage, onions, peppers, and, at lower elevations, sweet yucca, and arrowroot were grown extensively for export; indeed, so export-minded was the community that it was almost impossible to buy locally grown produce in the village. People couldn't be bothered with retail scales.

20. Why was there primitiveness and self-containment in Nayon before 1910? 20.__

A. Social mores
B. Cultural tradition
C. Biological instincts
D. Geographical factors
E. Religious regulations

21. By 1948, the village of Nayon was 21.__

A. a self-sufficient village
B. out of touch with the outside world
C. a small dependent portion of a larger economic unit
D. a rapidly growing and sound social and cultural unit
E. a metropolis

22. Why was Nayon originally separated from its neighbors? 22.__

A. Rich arable land
B. Long meandering streams
C. Artificial political barriers
D. Broad stretches of arid desert
E. Deep rugged gorges traversed by rock trails

TEST 19

Read the verse and fill in the space beside the object described in the verse.

I have two eyes and when I'm worn
I give the wearer four.
I'm strong or weak or thick or thin -
Need I say much more?

23. A. ___ Clock B. ___ Eyeglasses C. ___Piano 23.__
D. ___ Thermometer E. ___ I don't know

TEST 20

Scarlet fever begins with fever, chills, headache, and sore throat. A doctor diagnoses the illness as scarlet fever when a characteristic rash erupts on the skin. This rash appears on the neck and chest in three to five days after the onset of the illness and spreads rapidly over the body. Sometimes the skin on the palm of the hands and soles

of the feet shreds in flakes. Scarlet fever is usually treated with penicillin and, in severe cases, a convalescent serum. The disease may be accompanied by infections of the ear and throat, inflammation of the kidneys, pneumonia, and inflammation of the heart.

24. How does the author tell us that scarlet fever may be a serious disease? 24.____

A. He tells how many people die of it.
B. He tells that he once had the disease.
C. He tells that hands and feet may fall off.
D. He tells how other infections may come with scarlet fever.
E. None of the above

TEST 21

Read the verse and fill in the space beside the object described in the verse.

I have no wings but often fly:
I come in colors many.
From varied nationalities
Respect I get a-plenty.

25. A. ___ Deck of cards B. ___ Eyeglasses C. ___ Flag 25.____
D. ___ Needles E. ___ None of the above

KEY (CORRECT ANSWERS)

1. D
2. B
3. B
4. D
5. B

6. B
7. C
8. E
9. C
10. E

11. E
12. C
13. D
14. E
15. D

16. E
17. D
18. C
19. B
20. D

21. C
22. E
23. B
24. D
25. C

READING COMPREHENSION
UNDERSTANDING AND INTERPRETING WRITTEN MATERIAL
COMMENTARY

The ability to read and understand written materials -- texts, publications, newspapers, orders, directions, expositions -- is a skill basic to a functioning democracy and to an efficient business or viable government.

That is why almost all examinations -- for beginning, middle, and senior levels -- test reading comprehension, directly or indirectly.

The reading test measures how well you understand what you read. This is how it is done: You read a short paragraph and five statements. From the five statements, you choose the one statement, or answer, that is BEST supported by, or best matches, what is said in the paragraph.

SAMPLE QUESTIONS

DIRECTIONS: Each question has five suggested answers, lettered A,B,C,D, and E. Decide which one is the BEST answer. *PRINT THE LETTER OF THE CORRECT ANSWER IN THE SPACE AT THE RIGHT.*

1. The prevention of accidents makes it necessary not only that safety devices be used to guard exposed machinery but also that mechanics be instructed in safety rules which they must follow for their own protection and that the light in the plant be adequate.
The paragraph BEST supports the statement that industrial accidents
A. are always avoidable
B. may be due to ignorance
C. usually result from inadequate machinery
D. cannot be entirely overcome
E. result in damage to machinery

ANALYSIS

Remember what you have to do --
First - Read the paragraph.
Second - Decide what the paragraph means.
Third - Read the five suggested answers.
Fourth - Select the one answer which BEST matches what the paragraph says or is BEST supported by something in the paragraph. (Sometimes you may have to read the paragraph again in order to be sure which suggested answer is best.)

This paragraph is talking about three steps that should be taken to prevent industrial accidents --
1. use safety devices on machines
2. instruct mechanics in safety rules
3. provide adequate lighting.

SELECTION

With this in mind let's look at each suggested answer. Each one starts with "Industrial accidents ..."

SUGGESTED ANSWER A.

Industrial accidents (A) are always avoidable.
(The paragraph talks about how to avoid accidents, but does not say that accidents are always avoidable.)

SUGGESTED ANSWER B.

Industrial accidents (b) may be due to ignorance.

(One of the steps given in the paragraph to prevent accidents is to instruct mechanics on safety rules. This suggests that lack of knowledge or ignorance of safety rules causes accidents. This suggested answer sounds like a good possibility for being the right answer.)

SUGGESTED ANSWER C.

Industrial accidents (C) usually result from inadequate machinery.

(The paragraph does suggest that exposed machines cause accidents, but it doesn't say that it is the usual cause of accidents. The word *usually* makes this a wrong answer.)

SUGGESTED ANSWER D.

Industrial accidents (D) cannot be entirely overcome.

(You may know from your own experience that this is a true statement. But that is not what the paragraph is talking about. Therefore it is NOT the correct answer.)

SUGGESTED ANSWER E.

Industrial accidents (E) result in damage to machinery.

(This is a statement that may or may not be true, but in any case it is NOT covered by the paragraph.)

Looking back, you see that the one suggested answer of the five given that BEST matches what the paragraph says is --

Industrial accidents (B) may be due to ignorance.

The CORRECT answer then is B.

Be sure you read ALL the possible answers before you make your choice. You may think that none of the five answers is really good, but choose the BEST one of the five.

---

2. Probably few people realize, as they drive on a concrete road, that steel is used to keep the surface flat in spite of the weight of the busses and trucks. Steel bars, deeply embedded in the concrete, provide sinews to take the stresses so that the stresses cannot crack the slab or make it wavy.

   The paragraph BEST supports the statement THAT a concrete road

   A. is expensive to build
   B. usually cracks under heavy weights
   C. looks like any other road
   D. is used only for heavy traffic
   E. is reinforced with other material

ANALYSIS

This paragraph is commenting on the fact that --

1. few people realize, as they drive on a concrete road, that steel is deeply embedded
2. steel keeps the surface flat
3. steel bars enable the road to take the stresses without cracking or becoming wavy.

SELECTION

Now read and think about the possible answers:

A. A concrete road is expensive to build.
   (Maybe so but that is not what the paragraph is about.)

B. A concrete road usually cracks under heavy weights.
   (The paragraph talks about using steel bars to prevent heavy weights from cracking concrete roads. It says nothing about how usual it is for the roads to crack. The word *usually* makes this suggested answer wrong.)

C. A concrete road looks like any other road.
(This may or may not be true. The important thing to note is that it has nothing to do with what the paragraph is about.)

D. A concrete road is used only for heavy traffic.
(This answer at least has something to do with the paragraph -- concrete roads are used with heavy traffic but it does not say "used only.")

E. A concrete road is reinforced with other material.
(This choice seems to be the correct one on two counts: *First,* the paragraph does suggest that concrete roads are made stronger by embedding steel bars in them. This is another way of saying "concrete roads are reinforced with steel bars." *Second,* by the process of elimination, the other four choices are ruled out as correct answers simply because they do not apply.)

You can be sure that not all the reading questions will be so easy as these.

HINTS FOR ANSWERING READING QUESTIONS

1. Read the paragraph carefully. Then read each suggested answer carefully. Read every word, because often one word can make the difference between a right and a wrong answer.
2. Choose that answer which is supported in the paragraph itself. Do not choose an answer which is a correct statement unless it is based on information in the paragraph.
3. Even though a suggested answer has many of the words used in the paragraph, it may still be wrong.
4. Look out for words -- such as *always, never, entirely, or only* -- which tend to make a suggested answer wrong.
5. Answer first those questions which you can answer most easily. Then work on the other questions.
6. If you can't figure out the answer to the question, guess.

EXAMINATION SECTION

DIRECTIONS FOR THIS SECTION:
Each question has five suggested answers, lettered A to E. Decide which one is the BEST answer. *PRINT THE LETTER OF THE CORRECT ANSWER IN THE SPACE AT THE RIGHT.*

TEST 1

1. Some specialists are willing to give their services to the Government entirely free of charge; some feel that a nominal salary, such as will cover traveling expenses, is sufficient for a position that is recognized as being somewhat honorary in nature; many other specialists value their time so highly that they will not devote any of it to public service that does not repay them at a rate commensurate with the fees that they can obtain from a good private clientele. 1. ...
The paragraph BEST supports the statement that the use of specialists by the Government
   A. is rare because of the high cost of securing such persons
   B. may be influenced by the willingness of specialists to serve
   C. enables them to secure higher salaries in private fields
   D. has become increasingly common during the past few years
   E. always conflicts with private demands for their services

2. The fact must not be overlooked that only about one-half of the international trade of the world crosses the oceans. The other half is merely exchanges of merchandise between countries lying alongside each other or at least within the same continent. 2. ...
The paragraph BEST supports the statement that
   A. the most important part of any country's trade is transoceanic
   B. domestic trade is insignificant when compared with foreign trade
   C. the exchange of goods between neighborhing countries is not considered international trade
   D. foreign commerce is not necessarily carried on by water
   E. about one-half of the trade of the world is international
3. Individual differences in mental traits assume importance in fitting workers to jobs because such personal characteristics are persistent and are relatively little influenced by training and experience. 3. ...
The paragraph BEST supports the statement that training and experience
   A. are limited in their effectiveness in fitting workers to jobs
   B. do not increase a worker's fitness for a job
   C. have no effect upon a person's mental traits
   D. have relatively little effect upon the individual's chances for success
   E. should be based on the mental traits of an individual
4. The competition of buyers tends to keep prices up, the competition of sellers to send them down. Normally the pressure of competition among sellers is stronger than that among buyers since the seller has his article to sell and must get rid of it, whereas the buyer is not committed to anything. 4. ...
The paragraph BEST supports the statement that low prices are caused by
   A. buyer competition
   B. competition of buyers with sellers
   C. fluctuations in demand
   D. greater competition among sellers than among buyers
   E. more sellers than buyers
5. In seventeen states, every lawyer is automatically a member of the American Bar Association. In some other states and localities, truly representative organizations of the Bar have not yet come into being, but are greatly needed. 5. ...
The paragraph IMPLIES that
   A. representative Bar Associations are necessary in states where they do not now exist
   B. every lawyer is required by law to become a member of the Bar
   C. the Bar Association is a democratic organization
   D. some states have more lawyers than others
   E. every member of the American Bar Association is automatically a lawyer in seventeen states.

TEST 2

1. We hear a great deal about the new education, and see a great deal of it in action. But the school house, though prodigiously magnified in scale, is still very much the same old school house. 1. ...
   The paragraph IMPLIES that
   A. the old education was, after all, better than the new
   B. although the modern school buildings are larger than the old ones, they have not changed very much in other respects
   C. the old school houses do not fit in with modern educational theories
   D. a fine school building does not make up for poor teachers
   E. schools will be schools

2. No two human beings are of the same pattern --not even twins-- and the method of bringing out the best in each one necessarily varies according to the nature of the child. 2. ...
   The paragraph IMPLIES that
   A. individual differences should be considered in dealing with children
   B. twins should be treated impartially
   C. it is an easy matter to determine the special abilities of children
   D. a child's nature varies from year to year
   E. we must discover the general technique of dealing with children

3. Man inhabits today a world very different from that which encompassed even his parents and grandparents. It is a world geared to modern machinery - automobiles, airplanes, power plants; it is linked together and served by electricity. 3. ...
   The paragraph IMPLIES that
   A. the world has not changed much during the last few generations
   B. modern inventions and discoveries have brought about many changes in man's way of living
   C. the world is run more efficiently today than it was in our grandparents' time
   D. man is much happier today than he was a hundred years ago
   E. we must learn to see man as he truly is, underneath the veneers of man's contrivances

4. Success in any study depends largely upon the interest taken in that particular subject by the student. This being the case, each teacher earnestly hopes that her students will realize at the very outset that shorthand can be made an intensely fascinating study. 4. ...
   The paragraph IMPLIES that
   A. everyone is interested in shorthand
   B. success in a study is entirely impossible unless the student finds the study very interesting
   C. if a student is eager to study shorthand, he is likely to succeed in it
   D. shorthand is necessary for success
   E. anyone who is not interested in shorthand will not succeed in business

5. The primary purpose of all business English is to move the reader to agreeable and mutually profitable action. This action may be indirect or direct, but in either case a highly competitive appeal for business should be clothed with incisive diction tending to replace vagueness and doubt with clarity, confidence, and appropriate action. 5. ...
The paragraph IMPLIES that the
   A. ideal business letter uses words to conform to the reader's language level
   B. business correspondent should strive for conciseness in letter writing
   C. keen competition of today has lessened the value of the letter as an appeal for business
   D. writer of a business letter should employ incisive diction to move the reader to compliant and gainful action
   E. the writer of a business letter should be himself clear, confident, and forceful

TEST 3

1. To serve the community best, a comprehensive city plan must coordinate all physical improvements, even at the possible expense of subordinating individual desires, to the end that a city may grow in a more orderly way and provide adequate facilities for its people. 1. ...
The paragraph IMPLIES that
   A. city planning provides adequate facilities for recreation
   B. a comprehensive city plan provides the means for a city to grow in a more orderly fashion
   C. individual desires must always be subordinated to civic changes
   D. the only way to serve a community is to adopt a comprehensive city plan
   E. city planning is the most important function of city government
2. Facility in writing letters, the knack of putting into these quickly written letters the same personal impression that would mark an interview, and the ability to boil down to a one-page letter the gist of what might be called a five or ten minute conversation - all these are essential to effective work under conditions of modern business organization. 2. ...
The paragraph IMPLIES that
   A. letters are of more importance in modern business activities than ever before
   B. letters should be used in place of interviews
   C. the ability to write good letters is essential to effective work in modern business organization
   D. business letters should never be more than one page in length
   E. the person who can write a letter with great skill will get ahead more readily than others

3. The general rule is that it is the city council which determines the amount to be raised by taxation and which therefore determines, within the law, the tax rates. As has been pointed out, however, no city council or city authority has the power to determine what kinds of taxes should be levied. 3. ...
The paragraph IMPLIES that
   A. the city council has more authority than any other municipal body
   B. while the city council has a great deal of authority in the levying of taxes, its power is not absolute
   C. the kinds of taxes levied in different cities vary greatly
   D. the city council appoints the tax collectors
   E. the mayor determines the kinds of taxes to be levied
4. The growth of modern business has made necessary mass production, mass distribution, and mass selling. As a result, the problems of personnel and industrial relations have increased so rapidly that grave injustices in the handling of personal relationships have frequently occurred. Personnel administration is complex because, as in all human problems, many intangible elements are involved. Therefore a thorough, systematic, and continuous study of the psychology of human behavior is essential to the intelligent handling of personnel. 4. ...
The paragraph IMPLIES that
   A. complex modern industry makes impossible the personal relationships which formerly existed between employer and employee
   B. mass decisions are successfully applied to personnel problems
   C. the human element in personnel administration makes continuous study necessary to its intelligent application
   D. personnel problems are less important than the problems of mass production and mass distribution
   E. since personnel administration is so complex and costly, it should be subordinated to the needs of good industrial relations
5. The Social Security Act is striving toward the attainment of economic security for the individual and for his family. It was stated, in outlining this program, that security for the individual and for the family concerns itself with three factors: (1) decent homes to live in; (2) development of the natural resources of the country so as to afford the fullest opportunity to engage in productive work; and (3) safeguards against the major misfortunes of life. The Social Security Act is concerned with the third of these factors -"safeguards against misfortunes which cannot be wholly eliminated in this man-made world of ours." 5. ...
The paragraph IMPLIES that
   A. the Social Security Act is concerned primarily with supplying to families decent homes in which to live
   B. the development of natural resources is the only means of offering employment to the masses of the unemployed
   C. the Social Security Act has attained absolute economic security for the individual and for his family
   D. the Social Security Act deals with the first (1) factor as stated in the paragraph above
   E. the Social Security Act deals with the third (3) factor as stated in the paragraph above

TEST 4

PASSAGE 1

Free unrhymed verse has been practiced for some thousands of years and reaches back to the incantation which linked verse with the ritual dance. It provided a communal emotion; the aim of the cadenced phrases was to create a state of mind. The general coloring of free rhythms in the poetry of today is that of speech rhythm, composed in the sequence of the musical phrase, not in the sequence of the metronome, the regular beat. In the twenties, conventional rhyme fell into almost complete disuse. This liberation from rhyme became as well a liberation of rhyme. Freed of its exacting task of supporting lame verse, it would be applied with greater effect where wanted for some special effect. Such break in the tradition of rhymed verse had the healthy effect of giving it a fresh start, released from the hampering convention of too familiar cadences. This refreshing and subtilizing of the use of rhyme can be seen everywhere in the poetry today.

1. The title below that BEST expresses the ideas of this paragraph is: 1. ...
   A. Primitive poetry
   B. The origin of poetry
   C. Rhyme and rhythm in modern verse
   D. Classification of poetry
   E. Purposes in all poetry
2. Free verse had its origin in primitive 2. ...
   A. fairy tales B. literature C. warfare D. chants
   E. courtship
3. The object of early free verse was to 3. ...
   A. influence the mood of the people B. convey ideas
   C. produce mental pictures D. create pleasing sounds
   E. provide enjoyment

PASSAGE 2

Control of the Mississippi had always been goals of nations having ambitions in the New World. La Salle claimed it for France in 1682. Iberville appropriated it to France when he colonized Louisiana in 1700. Bienville founded New Orleans, its principal port, as a French city in 1718. The fleur-de-lis were the blazon of the delta country until 1762. Then Spain claimed all of Louisiana. The Spanish were easy neighbors. American products from western Pennsylvania and the Northwest Territory were barged down the Ohio and Mississippi to New Orleans, here they were reloaded on ocean-going vessels that cleared for the great seaports of the world.

1. The title below that BEST expresses the ideas of this paragraph is: 1. ...
   A. Importance of seaports
   B. France and Spain in the New World
   C. Early control of the Mississippi
   D. Claims of European nations
   E. American trade on the Mississippi
2. Until 1762 the lower Mississippi area was held by 2. ...
   A. England B. Spain C. the United States
   D. France E. Indians

3. In doing business with Americans the Spaniards were 3. ...
   A. easy to outsmart B. friendly to trade
   C. inclined to charge high prices for use of their ports
   D. shrewd E. suspicious

PASSAGE 3

Our humanity is by no means so materialistic as foolish talk is continually asserting it to be. Judging by what I have learned about men and women, I am convinced that there is far more in them of idealistic willpower than ever comes to the surface of the world. Just as the water of streams is small in amount compared to that which flows underground, so the idealism which becomes visible is small in amount compared with that which men and women bear locked in their hearts, unreleased or scarcely released. To unbind what is bound, to bring the underground waters to the surface -- mankind is waiting and longing for men who can do that.

1. The title below that BEST expresses the ideas of this paragraph is: 1. ...
   A. Releasing underground riches
   B. The good and bad in man
   C. Materialism in humanity
   D. The surface and the depths of idealism
   E. Unreleased energy
2. Human beings are more idealistic than 2. ...
   A. the water in underground streams
   B. their waiting and longing proves
   C. outward evidence shows
   D. the world
   E. other living creatures

PASSAGE 4

The total impression made by any work of fiction cannot be rightly understood without a sympathetic perception of the artistic aims of the writer. Consciously or unconsciouly, he has accepted certain facts, and rejected or suppressed other facts, in order to give unity to the particular aspect of human life which he is depicting. No novelist possesses the impartiality, the indifference, the infinite tolerance of nature. Nature displays to use, with complete unconcern, the beautiful and the ugly, the precious and the trivial, the pure and the impure. But a writer must select the aspects of nature and human nature which are demanded by the work in hand. He is forced to select, to combine, to create.

1. The title below that BEST expresses the ideas of this paragraph is: 1. ...
   A. Impressionists in literature
   B. Nature as an artist
   C. The novelist as an imitator
   D. Creative technic of the novelist
   E. Aspects of nature
2. A novelist rejects some facts because they 2. ...
   A. are impure and ugly
   B. would show he is not impartial
   C. are unrelated to human nature
   D. would make a bad impression
   E. mar the unity of his story

3. It is important for a reader to know 3. ...
   A. the purpose of the author
   B. what facts the author omits
   C. both the ugly and the beautiful
   D. something about nature
   E. what the author thinks of human nature

PASSAGE 5

If you watch a lamp which is turned very rapidly on and off, and you keep your eyes open, "persistence of vision" will bridge the gaps of darkness between the flashes of light, and the lamp will seem to be continuously lit. This "topical afterglow" explains the magic produced by the stroboscope, a new instrument which seems to freeze the swiftest motions while they are still going on, and to stop time itself dead in its tracks. The "magic" is all in the eye of the beholder.

1. The "magic" of the stroboscope is due to 1. ...
   A. continuous lighting B. intense cold
   C. slow motion D. behavior of the human eye
   E. a lapse of time
2. "Persistence of vision" is explained by 2. ...
   A. darkness B. winking C. rapid flashes
   D. gaps E. after impression

TEST 5

PASSAGE 1

During the past fourteen years, thousands of top-lofty United States elms have been marked for death by the activities of the tiny European elm bark beetle. The beetles, however, do not do fatal damage. Death is caused by another importation, Dutch elm disease, a fungus infection which the beetles carry from tree to tree. Up to 1941, quarantine and tree-sanitation measures kept the beetles and the disease pretty well confined within 510 miles around metropolitan New York. War curtailed these measures and made Dutch elm disease a wider menace. Every household and village that prizes an elm-shaded lawn or commons must now watch for it. Since there is as yet no cure for it, the infected trees must be pruned or felled, and the wood must be burned in order to protect other healthy trees.

1. The title below that BEST expresses the ideas of this paragraph is: 1. ...
   A. A menace to our elms B. Pests and diseases of the elm
   C. Our vanishing elms D. The need to protect Dutch elms
   E. How elms are protected
2. The danger of spreading the Dutch elm disease was increased by 2. ...
   A. destroying infected trees B. the war
   C. the lack of a cure D. a fungus infection
   E. quarantine measures
3. The European elm bark beetle is a serious threat to our elms because it 3. ...
   A. chews the bark B. kills the trees
   C. is particularly active on the eastern seaboard
   D. carries infection E. cannot be controlled

PASSAGE 2

It is elemental that the greater the development of man, the greater the problems he has to concern him. When he lived in a cave with stone implements, his mind no less than his actions was grooved into simple channels. Every new invention, every new way of doing things posed fresh problems for him. And, as he moved along the road, he questioned each step, as indeed he should, for he trod upon the beliefs of his ancestors. It is equally elemental to say that each step upon this later road posed more questions than the earlier ones. It is only the edcated man who realizes the results of his actions; it is only the thoughtful one who questions his own decisions.

1. The title below that BEST expresses the ideas of this paragraph is: 1. ...
   - A. Channels of civilization
   - B. The mark of a thoughtful man
   - C. The cave man in contrast with man today
   - D. The price of early progress
   - E. Man's never-ending challenge

PASSAGE 3

Spring is one of those things that man has no hand in, any more than he has a part in sunrise or the phases of the moon. Spring came before man was here to enjoy it, and it will go right on coming even if man isn't here some time in the future. It is a matter of solar mechanics and celestial order. And for all our knowledge of astronomy and terrestrial mechanics, we haven't yet been able to do more than bounce a radar beam off the moon. We couldn't alter the arrival of the spring equinox by as much as one second, if we tried.

Spring is a matter of growth, of chlorophyll, of bud and blossom. We can alter growth and change the time of blossoming in individual plants; but the forests still grow in nature's way, and the grass of the plains hasn't altered its nature in a thousand years. Spring is a magnificent phase of the cycle of nature; but man really hasn't any guiding or controlling hand in it. He is here to enjoy it and benefit by it. And April is a good time to realize it; by May perhaps we will want to take full credit.

1. The title below that BEST expresses the ideas of this passage is: 1. ...
   - A. The marvels of the Spring equinox
   - B. Nature's dependence on mankind
   - C. The weakness of man opposed to nature
   - D. The glories of the world
   - E. Eternal growth
2. The author of the passage states that 2. ...
   - A. man has a part in the phases of the moon
   - B. April is a time for taking full-credit
   - C. April is a good time to enjoy nature
   - D. man has a guiding hand in spring
   - E. spring will cease to be if civilization ends

PASSAGE 4

The walled medieval town was as characteristic of its period as the cut of a robber baron's beard. It sprang out of the exigencies of war, and it was not without its architectural charm, whatever its hygienic deficiencies may have been. Behind its high, thick walls not only the normal inhabitants but the whole countryside fought and cowered in an hour of need. The capitals of Europe now forsake the city when the sirens scream and death from the sky seems imminent. Will the fear of bombs accelerate the slow decentralization which began with the automobile and the wide distribution of electrical energy and thus reverse the medieval flow to the city?

1. The title below that BEST expresses the ideas in this paragraph is. 1. ...
   A. A changing function of the town B. The walled medieval town
   C. The automobile's influence on city life D. Forsaking the city
   E. Bombs today and yesterday
2. Conditions in the Middle Ages made the walled town 2. ...
   A. a natural development B. the most dangerous of all places
   C. a victim of fires D. lacking in architectural charm
   E. healthful
3. Modern conditions may 3. ...
   A. make cities larger B. make cities more hygienic
   C. protect against floods
   D. cause people to move from population centers
   E. encourage good architecture

PASSAGE 5

The literary history of this nation began when the first settler from abroad of sensitive mind paused in his adventure long enough to feel that he was under a different sky, breathing new air, and that a New World was all before him with only his strength and Providence for guides. With him began a new emphasis upon an old theme in literature, the theme of cutting loose and faring forth, renewed, under the powerful influence of a fresh continent for civilized man. It has provided, ever since those first days, a strong current in our native literature, whose other flow has come from a nostalgia for the rich culture of Europe, so much of which was perforce left behind.

1. The title below that BEST expresses the ideas of this paragraph is: 1. ...
   A. America's distinctive literature B. Pioneer authors
   C. The dead hand of the past D. Europe's literary grandchild
   E. America comes of age
2. American writers, according to the author, because of their colonial experiences 2. ...
   A. were antagonistic to European writers
   B. cut loose from Old World influences
   C. wrote only on New World events and characters
   D. created new literary themes
   E. gave fresh interpretation to an old literary idea

TEST 6

1. Any business not provided with capable substitutes to fill all important positions is a weak business. Therefore a foreman should train each man not only to perform his own particular duties but also to do those of two or three positions. 1. ...
The paragraph BEST supports the statement that
   A. dependence on substitutes is a sign of weak organization
   B. training will improve the strongest organization
   C. the foreman should be the most expert at any particular job under him
   D. every employee can be trained to perform efficiently work other than his own
   E. vacancies in vital positions should be provided for in advance

2. The coloration of textile fabrics composed of cotton and wool generally requires two processes, as the process used in dyeing wool is seldom capable of fixing the color upon cotton. The usual method is to immerse the fabric in the requisite baths to dye the wool and then to treat the partially dyed material in the manner found suitable for cotton. 2. ...
The paragraph BEST supports the statement that the dyeing of textile fabrics composed of cotton and wool
   A. is less complicated than the dyeing of wool alone
   B. is more successful when the material contains more cotton than wool
   C. is not satisfactory when solid colors are desired
   D. is restricted to two colors for any one fabric
   E. is usually based upon the methods required for dyeing the different materials

3. The serious investigator must direct his whole effort toward success in his work. If he wishes to succeed in each investigation, his work will be by no means easy, smooth, or peaceful; on the contrary, he will have to devote himself completely and continuously to a task that requires all his ability. 3. ...
The paragraph BEST supports the statement that an investigator's success depends most upon
   A. ambition to advance rapidly in the service
   B. persistence in the face of difficulty
   C. training and experience
   D. willingness to obey orders without delay
   E. the number of investigations which he conducts

4. Honest people in one nation find it difficult to understand the viewpoint of honest people in another. State departments and their ministers exist for the purpose of explaining the viewpoints of one nation in terms understood by another. Some of their most important work lies in this direction. 4. ...
The paragraph BEST supports the statement that
   A. people of different nations may not consider matters in the same light
   B. it is unusual for many people to share similar ideas
   C. suspicion prevents understanding between nations
   D. the chief work of state departments is to guide relations between nations united by a common cause
   E. the people of one nation must sympathize with the viewpoints of others

5. Economy once in a while is just not enough. I expect to find it at every level of responsibility, from cabinet member to the newest and youngest recruit. Controlling waste is something like bailing a boat; you have to keep at it. I have no intention of easing up on my insistence on getting a dollar of value for each dollar we spend. 5. ...
The paragraph BEST supports the statement that
   A. we need not be concerned about items which cost less than a dollar
   B. it is advisable to buy the cheaper of two items
   C. the responsibility of economy is greater at high levels than at low levels
   D. economy becomes easy with practice
   E. economy is a continuing responsibility

TEST 7

1. On all permit imprint mail the charge for postage has been printed by the mailer before he presents it for mailing and pays the postage. Such mail of any class is mailable only at the post office that issued a permit covering it. Since the postage receipts for such mail represent only the amount of permit imprint mail detected and verified, employees in receiving, handling, and outgoing sections must be alert constantly to route such mail to the weighing section before it is handled or dispatched. 1. ...
The paragraph BEST supports the statement that, at post offices where permit mail is received for dispatch,
   A. dispatching units make a final check on the amount of postage payable on permit imprint mail
   B. employees are to check the postage chargeable on mail received under permit
   C. neither more nor less postage is to be collected than the amount printed on permit imprint mail
   D. the weighing section is primarily responsible for failure to collect postage on such mail
   E. unusual measures are taken to prevent unstamped mail from being accepted
2. Education should not stop when the individual has been prepared to make a livelihood and to live in modern society. Living would be mere existence were there no appreciation and enjoyment of the riches of art, literature, and science. 2. ...
The paragraph BEST supports the statement that true education
   A. is focused on the routine problems of life
   B. prepares one for full enjoyment of life
   C. deals chiefly with art, literature and science
   D. is not possible for one who does not enjoy scientific literature
   E. disregards practical ends
3. Insured and c.o.d. air and surface mail is accepted with the understanding that the sender guarantees any necessary forwarding or return postage. When such mail is forwarded or returned, it shall be rated up for collection of postage; except that insured or c.o.d. air mail weighing 8 ounces or less 3. ...

and subject to the 40 cents an ounce rate shall be forwarded by air if delivery will be advanced, and returned by surface means, without additional postage.
The paragraph BEST supports the statement that the return postage for undeliverable insured mail is
A. included in the original prepayment on air mail parcels
B. computed but not collected before dispatching surface patrol post mail to sender
C. not computed or charged for any air mail that is returned by surface transportation
D. included in the amount collected when the sender mails parcel post
E. collected before dispatching for return if any amount due has been guaranteed

4. All undeliverable first-class mail, except first-class parcels and parcel post paid with first-class postage, which cannot be returned to the sender, is sent to a dead-letter branch. Undeliverable matter of the third-and fourth-classes of obvious value for which the sender does not furnish return postage and undeliverable first-class parcels and parcel-post matter bearing postage of the first-class, which cannot be returned, is sent to a dead parcel-post branch. 4. ...
The paragraph BEST supports the statement that matter that is sent to a dead parcel-post branch includes all undeliverable
A. mail, except first-class letter mail, that appears to be valuable
B. mail, except that of the first-class, on which the sender failed to prepay the original mailing costs
C. parcels on which the mailer prepaid the first-class rate of postage
D. third- and fourth-class matter on which the required return postage has not been paid
E. parcels on which first-class postage has been prepaid, when the sender's address is not known

5. Civilization started to move rapidly when man freed himself of the shackles that restricted his search for truth. 5. ...
The paragraph BEST supports the statement that the progress of civilization
A. came as a result of man's dislike for obstacles
B. did not begin until restrictions on learning were removed
C. has been aided by man's efforts to find the truth
D. is based on continually increasing efforts
E. continues at a constantly increasing rate

TEST 8

1. Telegrams should be clear, concise, and brief. Omit all unnecessary words. The parts of speech most often used in telegrams are nouns,verbs,adjectives,and adverbs. If possible,do without pronouns,prepositions,articles,and copulative verbs. Use simple sentences, rather than complex and compound. 1. ...
The paragraph BEST supports the statement that in writing telegrams one should always use
A. common and simple words

B. only nouns,verbs,adjectives,and adverbs
C. incomplete sentences
D. only words essential to the meaning
E. the present tense of verbs

2. The function of business is to increase the wealth of the country and the value and happiness of life. It does this by supplying the material needs of men and women. When the nation's business is successfully carried on, it renders public service of the highest value. 2. ...
The paragraph BEST supports the statement that
A. all businesses which render public service are successful
B. human happiness is enhanced only by the increase of material wants
C. the value of life is increased only by the increase of wealth
D. the material needs of men and women are supplied by well-conducted business
E. business is the only field of activity which increases happiness

3. In almost every community, fortunately, there are certain men and women known to be public-spirited. Others, however, may be selfish and act only as their private interests seem to require. 3. ...
The paragraph BEST supports the statement that those citizens who disregard others are
A. fortunate
B. needed
C. found only in small communities
D. not known
E. not public-spirited

KEY (CORRECT ANSWERS)

TEST 1
1. B
2. D
3. A
4. D
5. A

TEST 2
1. B
2. A
3. B
4. C
5. D

TEST 3
1. B
2. C
3. B
4. C
5. E

TEST 4
PASSAGE 1
1. C
2. D
3. A
PASSAGE 2
1. C
2. D
3. B
PASSAGE 3
1. D
2. C
PASSAGE 4
1. D
2. E
2. A
PASSAGE 5
1. D
2. E

TEST 5
PASSAGE 1
1. A
2. B
3. D
PASSAGE 2
1. E
PASSAGE 3
1. C
2. C
PASSAGE 4
1. A
2. A
3. D
PASSAGE 5
1. A
2. E

TEST 6
1. E
2. E
3. B
4. A
5. E

TEST 7
1. B
2. B
3. B
4. E
5. C

TEST 8
1. D
2. D
3. E

READING COMPREHENSION
UNDERSTANDING WRITTEN MATERIALS

COMMENTARY

The ability to read and understand written materials – texts, publications, newspapers, orders, directions, expositions – is a skill basic to a functioning democracy and to an efficient business or viable government.

That is why almost all examinations – for beginning, middle, and senior levels – test reading comprehension, directly or indirectly.

The reading test measures how well you understand what you read. This is how it is done: You read a passage followed by several statements. From these statements, you choose the *one* statement, or answer, that is BEST supported by, or BEST matches, what is said in the paragraph. *PRINT THE LETTER OF THE CORRECT ANSWER IN THE SPACE AT THE RIGHT.*

SAMPLE QUESTION

DIRECTIONS: Answer Question 1 ONLY according to the information given in the following passage :

1. A cashier has to make many arithmetic calculations in connection with his work. Skill in arithmetic comes readily with practice; no special talent is needed. 1.____
On the basis of the above statement, it is MOST accurate to state that

    A. the most important part of a cashier's job is to make calculations
    B. few cashiers have the special ability needed to handle arithmetic problems easily
    C. without special talent, cashiers cannot learn to do the calculations they are required to do in their work
    D. a cashier can, with practice, learn to handle the computations he is required to make.

    The *correct* answer is D.

EXAMINATION SECTION
TEST 1

Questions 1-5.

DIRECTIONS: Questions 1 to 5 are based on the following reading passage:

The size of each collection route will be determined by the amount of waste per stop, distance between stops, speed of loading, speed of truck, traffic conditions during loading time, etc.

Basically, the route should consist of a proper amount of work for a crew for the daily working period. The crew should service all properties eligible for this service in their area. Routes should, whenever practical, be compact, with a logical progression through the area. Unnecessary travel should be avoided. Traffic conditions on the route should be thoroughly studied to prevent lost time in loading, to reduce hazards to employees, and to minimize tying up of regular traffic movements by collection forces. Natural and physical barriers and arterial streets should be used as route boundaries wherever possible to avoid lost time in travel.

Routes within a district should be laid out so that the crews start at the point farthest from the disposal area and, as the day progresses, move toward that area, thus reducing the length of the haul. When possible, the work of the crews in a district should be parallel as they progress throughout the day, with routes finishing up within a short distance of each other. This enables the supervisor to be present when crews are completing their work and enables him to shift crews to trouble spots to complete the day's work.

1. Based on the above passage, an advantage of having collection routes end near one another is that 1._

   A. routes can be made more compact
   B. unnecessary travel is avoided, saving manpower
   C. the length of the haul is reduced
   D. the supervisor can exercise better manpower control

2. Of the factors mentioned above which affect the size of a collection route, the two over which the sanitation forces have LEAST control are 2._

   A. amount of waste; traffic conditions
   B. speed of loading; amount of waste
   C. speed of truck; distance between stops
   D. traffic conditions; speed of truck

3. According to the above passage, the size of a collection route is probably good if 3._

   A. it is a fair day's work for a normal crew
   B. it is not necessary for the trucks to travel too fast
   C. the amount of waste collected can be handled properly
   D. the distance between stops is approximately equal

4. Based on the above passage, it is reasonable to assume that a sanitation officer laying out collection routes should NOT try to have 4.____

   A. an arterial street as a route boundary
   B. any routes near the disposal area
   C. the routes overlap a little
   D. the routes run in the same direction

5. The term "logical progression" as used in the second paragraph of the passage refers MOST nearly to 5.____

   A. collecting from street after street in order
   B. numbering streets one after the other
   C. rotating crew assignments
   D. using logic as a basis for assignment of crews

TEST 2

Questions 1-3.

DIRECTIONS: Answer Questions 1, 2, and 3 *SOLELY* on the basis of the paragraph below.

In an open discussion designed to arrive at solutions to community problems, the person leading the discussion group should give the members a chance to make their suggestions before he makes his. He must not be afraid of silence, if he talks just to keep things going, he will find he can't stop, and good discussion will not develop. In other words, the more he talks, the more the group will depend on him. If he finds, however, that no one seems ready to begin the discussion, his best "opening" is to ask for definitions of terms which form the basis of the discussion. By pulling out as many definitions or interpretations as possible, he can get the group started "thinking out loud," which is essential to good discussion.

1. According to the above paragraph, good group discussion is *most likely* to result if the person leading the discussion group 1._

    A. keeps the discussion going by speaking whenever the group stops speaking
    B. encourages the group to depend on him by speaking more than any other group member
    C. makes his own suggestions before the group has a chance to make theirs
    D. encourages discussion by asking the group to interpret the terms to be discussed

2. According to the paragraph above, "thinking out loud" by the discussion group is 2._

    A. *good* practice, because "thinking out loud" is important to good discussion
    B. *poor* practice, because group members should think out their ideas before discussing them
    C. *good* practice, because it will encourage the person leading the discussion to speak more
    D. *poor* practice, because it causes the group to fear silence during a discussion

3. According to the paragraph above, the *one* of the following which is **LEAST** desirable at an open discussion is having 3._

    A. silent periods during which none of the group members speaks
    B. differences of opinion among the group members concerning the definition of terms
    C. a discussion leader who uses "openings" to get the discussion started
    D. a discussion leader who provides all suggestions and definitions for the group

TEST 3

Questions 1-4.

DIRECTIONS: Questions 1 through 4 are to be answered *SOLELY* on the basis of the following information.

The insects you will control are just a minute fraction of the millions which inhabit the world. Man does well to hold his own in the face of the constant pressures that insects continue to exert upon him. Not only are the total numbers tremendous, but the number of individual kinds, or species, certainly exceeds 800,000 – number greater than that of all other animals combined. Many of these are beneficial but some are especially competitive with man. Not only are insects numerous, but they are among he most adaptable of all animals. In their many forms, they are fitted for almost any specific way of life. Their adaptability, combined with their tremendous rate of reproduction, gives insects an unequaled potential for survival!

The food of insects includes almost anything that can be eaten by any other animal as well as many things which cannot even be digested by any other animals. Most insects do not harm the products of man or carry diseases harmful to him; however many do carry diseases and others feed on his food and manufactured goods. Some are adapted to living only in open areas while others are able to live in extremely confined spaces. All of these factors combined make the insects a group of animals having many members which are a nuisance to man and thus of great importance.

The control of insects requires an understanding of their way of life. Thus it is necessary to understand the anatomy of the insect, its method of growth, the time it takes for the insect to grow from egg to adult, its habits, the stage of its life history in which it causes damage, its food, and its common living places. In order to obtain the best control, it is especially important to be able to identify correctly the specific insect involved because, without this knowledge, it is impossible to prescribe a proper treatment.

1. Which one of the following is a CORRECT statement about the insect population of the world, according to the above paragraph? The 1.____

   A. total number of insects is less than the total number of all other animals combined
   B. number of species of insects is greater than the number of species of all other animals combined
   C. total number of harmful insects is greater than the total number of those which are not harmful
   D. number of species of harmless insects is less than the number of species of those which are harmful

2. Insects will be controlled MOST efficiently if you 2.____

   A. understand why the insects are so numerous
   B. know what insects you are dealing with
   C. see if the insects compete with man
   D. are able to identify the food which the insects digest

3. According to the above passage, insects are of importance to a scientist **PRIMARILY** because they 3._

   A. can be annoying, destructive, and harmful to man
   B. are able to thrive in very small spaces
   C. cause damage during their growth stages
   D. are so adaptable that they can adjust to any environment

4. According to the above passage, insects can eat 4.__

   A. everything that any other living thing can eat
   B. man's food and things which he makes
   C. anything which other animals can't digest
   D. only food and food products

TEST 4

Questions 1-4.

DIRECTIONS: Answer Questions 1 through 4 on the basis of the information given in the following passage.

Telephone service in a government agency should be adequate and complete with respect to information given or action taken. It must be remembered that telephone contacts should receive special consideration since the caller cannot see the operator. People like to feel that they are receiving personal attention and that their requests or criticisms are receiving individual rather than routine consideration. All this contributes to what has come to be known as *tone of service*. The aim is to use standards which are clearly very good or superior. The factors to be considered in determining what makes good tone of service are speech, courtesy, understanding and explanations. A caller's impression of tone of service will affect the general public attitude toward the agency and city services in general.

1. The above passage states that people who telephone a government agency like to feel that they are 1._____

   A. creating a positive image of themselves
   B. being given routine consideration
   C. receiving individual attention
   D. setting standards for telephone service

2. Which of the following is NOT mentioned in the above passage as a factor in determining good tone of service? 2._____

   A. Courtesy B. Education C. Speech D. Understanding

3. The above passage implies that failure to properly handle telephone calls is *most likely* to result in 3._____

   A. a poor impression of city agencies by the public
   B. a deterioration of courtesy toward operators
   C. an effort by operators to improve the Tone of Service
   D. special consideration by the public of operator difficulties

TEST 5

Questions 1-5.

DIRECTIONS: Answer Questions 1 through 5 only on the basis of the information provided in the following passage:

For some office workers it is useful to be familiar with the four main classes of domestic mail; for others it is essential. Each class has a different rate of postage and some have requirements concerning wrapping, sealing or special information to be placed on the package.

First-class mail, the class which may not be opened for postal inspection, includes letters, post cards, business reply cards, and other kinds of written matter. There are different rates for some of the kinds of cards which can be sent by first-class mail. The maximum weight for an item sent by first-class mail is 70 pounds. An item which is not letter size should be marked "First Class" on all sides.

Although office workers most often come into contact with first-class mail, they may find it helpful to know something about the other classes. Second-class mail is generally used for mailing newspapers and magazines. Publishers of these articles must meet certain U. S. Postal Service requirements in order to obtain a permit to use second-class mailing rates. Third-class mail, which must weigh less than 1 pound, includes printed materials and merchandise parcels. There are two rate structures for this class, a single-piece rate and a bulk rate. Fourth-class mail, also known as parcel post, includes packages weighing from one to 40 pounds. For more information about these classes of mail and the actual mailing rates, contact your local post office.

1. According to this passage, first-class mail is the only class which 1._

   A. has a limit on the maximum weight of an item
   B. has different rates for items within the class
   C. may not be opened for postal inspection
   D. should be used by office workers

2. According to this passage, the one of the following items which may CORRECTLY be sent by fourth-class mail is a 2._

   A. magazine weighing one-half pound
   B. package weighing one-half pound
   C. package weighing two pounds
   D. post card

3. According to this passage, there are different postage rates for 3._

   A. a newspaper sent by second-class mail and a magazine sent by second-class mail
   B. each of the classes of mail
   C. each pound of fourth-class mail
   D. printed material sent by third-class mail and merchandise parcels sent by third-class mail

4. In order to send a newspaper by second-class mail, a publisher must 4._____

   A. have met certain postal requirements and obtained a permit
   B. indicate whether he wants to use the single-piece or the bulk rate
   C. make certain that the newspaper weighs less than one pound
   D. mark the newspaper "Second Class" on the top and bottom of the wrapper

5. Of the following types of information the one which is NOT mentioned in the passage is the 5._____

   A. class of mail to which parcel post belongs
   B. kinds of items which can be sent by each class of mail
   C. maximum weight for an item sent by fourth-class mail
   D. postage rate for each of the four classes of mail

TEST 6

Questions 1-5.

DIRECTIONS: Questions numbered 1 to 5 inclusive are to be answered in accordance with the following paragraph.

The thickness of insulation necessary for the most economical results varies with the steam temperature. The standard covering consists of 85 percent magnesia with 10 percent of long-fibre asbestos as a binder. Both matnesia and laminated asbestos-felt and other forms of mineral wool including glass wool are also used for heat insulation. The magnesia and laminated-asbestos coverings may be safely used at temperatures up to 600° F. Pipe insulation is applie d in molded sections 3 feet long; the sections are attached to the pipe by means of galvanized iron wire or netting. Flanges and fittings can be insulated by direct application of magnesia cement to the metal without *reinforcement.* Insulation should always be maintained in good condition because it saves fuel. Routine maintenance of warm-pipe insulation should include prompt repair of damaged surfaces. Steam and hot-water leaks concealed by insulation will be difficult to detect. Underground steam or hot-water pipes are best insulated using a concrete trench with removable cover.

1. The word *reinforcement*, as used above, means, most nearly, 1._

   A. resistance B. strengthening C. regulation D. removal

2. According to the above paragraph, magnesia and laminated asbestos coverings may be *safely* used at temperatures up to 2._

   A. 800° F B. 720° F C. 675° F D. 600° F

3. According to the above paragraph, insulation should *always* be maintained in good condition because it 3._

   A. is laminated
   B. saves fuel
   C. is attached to the pipe
   D. prevents leaks

4. According to the above paragraph, pipe insulation sections are attached to the pipe by means of 4._

   A. binders
   B. mineral wool
   C. netting
   D. staples

5. According to the above paragraph, a leak in a hot-water pipe may be difficult to detect because, when insulation is used, the leak is 5._

   A. underground
   B. hidden
   C. routine
   D. cemented

TEST 7

Questions 1-4.

DIRECTIONS: Questions 1 to 4 inclusive are to be answered *only* in accordance with the following paragraph.

Cylindrical surfaces are the most common form of finished surfaces found on machine parts, although flat surfaces are also very common; hence, many metal-cutting *processes* are for the purpose of producing either cylindrical or flat surfaces. The machines used for cylindrical or flat shapes may be, and often are, utilized also for forming the various irregular or special shapes required on many machine parts. Because of the prevalence of cylindrical and flat surfaces, the student of manufacturing practice should learn first about the machines and methods employed to produce these surfaces. The cylindrical surfaces may be internal as in holes and cylinders. Any one part may, of course, have cylindrical sections of different diameters and lengths and include flat ends or shoulders and, frequently, there is a threaded part or, possibly, some finished surface that is not circular in cross-section. The prevalence of cylindrical surfaces on machine parts explains why lathes are found in all machine shops. It is important to understand the various uses of the lathe because many of the operations are the same fundamentally as those performed on other types of machine tools.

1. According to the above paragraph, the *most common* form of finished surfaces found on machine parts is 1.____

   A. cylindrical B. elliptical
   C. flat D. square

2. According to the above paragraph, *any one* part of cylindrical surfaces may have 2.____

   A. chases B. shoulders C. keyways D. splines

3. According to the above paragraph, lathes are found in all machine shops because cylindrical surfaces on machine parts are 3.____

   A. scarce B. internal C. common D. external

4. As used in the above paragraph, the word *processes* means 4.____

   A. operations B. purposes C. devices D. tools

TEST 8

Questions 1-2.

DIRECTIONS: Questions 1 and 2 are to be answered in accordance with the following paragraph.

The principle of interchangeability requires manufacture to such specification that component parts of a device may be selected at random and assembled to fit and operate satisfactorily. Interchangeable manufacture, therefore, requires that parts be made to definite limits of error, and to fit gages instead of mating parts. Interchangeability does not necessarily involve a high degree of precision; stove lids, for example, are interchangeable but are not particularly accurate, and carriage bolts and nuts are not precision products but are completely interchangeable. Interchangeability may be employed in unit-production as well as mass-production systems of manufacture.

1. According to the above paragraph, in order for parts to be interchangeable, they must be 1.___

   A. precision-machined B. selectively-assembled
   C. mass-produced D. made to fit gages

2. According to the above paragraph, carriage bolts are interchangeable because they are 2.___

   A. precision-made
   B. sized to specific tolerances
   C. individually matched products
   D. produced in small units

KEY (CORRECT ANSWERS)

TEST 1	TEST 2	TEST 3	TEST 4	TEST 5	TEST 6	TEST 7	TEST 8
1. D	1. D	1. B	1. C	1. C	1. B	1. A	1. D
2. A	2. A	2. B	2. B	2. C	2. D	2. B	2. B
3. A	3. D	3. A	3. A	3. B	3. B	3. C	
4. C		4. B		4. A	4. C	4. A	
5. A				5. D	5. B		

READING COMPREHENSION
UNDERSTANDING AND INTERPRETING WRITTEN MATERIAL
EXAMINATION SECTION
TEST 1

DIRECTIONS: Each question or incomplete statement is followed by several suggested answers or completions. Select the one that BEST answers the question or completes the statement. *PRINT THE LETTER OF THE CORRECT ANSWER IN THE SPACE AT THE RIGHT.*

Questions 1-3.

DIRECTIONS: Questions 1 through 3 are to be answered SOLELY on the basis of the following paragraph.

Accident proneness is a subject which deserves much more objective and competent study than it has received to date. In discussing accident proneness, it is important to differentiate between the employee who is a *repeater* and one who is truly accident-prone. It is obvious that any person put on work of which he knows little without thorough training in safe practice for the work in question will be liable to injury until he does learn the *how* of it. Few workmen left to their own devices will develop adequate safe practices. Therefore, they must be trained. Only those who fail to respond to proper training should be regarded as accident-prone. The repeater whose accident record can be explained by a correctible physical defect, by correctible plant or machine hazards, by assignment to work for which he is not suited because of physical deficiencies or special abilities, cannot be fairly called *accident prone.*

1. According to the above paragraph, a person is considered accident prone if 1.____

   A. he has accidents regardless of the fact that he has been properly trained
   B. he has many accidents
   C. it is possible for him to have accidents
   D. he works at a job where accidents are possible

2. According to the above paragraph, 2.____

   A. workers will learn the safe way of doing things if left to their own intelligence
   B. most workers must be trained to be safe
   C. a worker who has had more than one accident has not been properly trained
   D. intelligent workers are always safe

3. According to the above paragraph, a person would not be called accident prone if the cause of his accident was 3.____

   A. a lack of interest in the job
   B. recklessness
   C. a low level of intelligence
   D. eyeglasses that don't fit properly

Questions 4-9.

DIRECTIONS: Each question consists of a statement. You are to indicate whether the statement is TRUE (T) or FALSE (F). Questions 4 through 9 are to be answered SOLELY on the basis of the following passage;

Every accident should be reported even though the accident seems very unimportant. The man involved may be unharmed, yet it is necessary in the case of all accidents to forward a written report containing all the facts that show how the accident occurred, including the time and place. The reason for this action is that a situation which does not cause injury at one time may cause serious injury at another time. A written report informs the safety director of a dangerous condition and helps his investigation by supplying important facts. He can, therefore, take steps to eliminate the hazard,

4. Only serious accidents should be reported. 4

5. If the man involved in an accident is unharmed, it is not necessary to send through a report. 5

6. An accident report should show how the accident happened and include the time and place of the accident. 6

7. A situation which does not cause an injury at one time cannot cause serious injury at another time. 7

8. When a written report of an accident is made, it means that the safety director is informed of a dangerous condition. 8

9. The facts in an accident report do not help the safety director in his investigation of the accident. 9

Questions 10-17.

DIRECTIONS: Each question consists of a statement. You are to indicate whether the statement is TRUE (T) or FALSE (F). Questions 10 through 17 are to be answered SOLELY on the basis of the following passage.

The Mayor is in charge of the city government. He has his office in City Hall in downtown. There are city rules, or laws, that all citizens must obey. For example, there is a law that no one can throw things on the sidewalks or into the streets. We want our city to be clean and beautiful. There are also traffic laws for the automobiles that use our city streets. For instance, the cars cannot go at more than a certain speed. The drivers must stop when the traffic lights turn red.

If people do not obey these rules or city laws, a policeman may arrest them. These laws were made to protect other people who want to use the streets too.

10. The head of the city government is the Mayor. 10

11. The Mayor's office is in the Municipal Building. 11

12. The Mayor does not have to obey the city laws or rules. 12._____

13. Anyone who throws things on the sidewalks is breaking the law. 13._____

14. There is a traffic law that does not allow a car to go faster than a certain speed. 14._____

15. A driver does not have to stop when the traffic lights turn red. 15._____

16. A policeman may arrest a driver who does not obey the traffic laws. 16._____

17. People who use the streets are not protected by the traffic laws. 17._____

Questions 18-25.

DIRECTIONS: Each question consists of a statement. You are to indicate whether the statement is TRUE (T) or FALSE (F). Questions 18 through 25 are to be answered SOLELY on the basis of the following passage.

NEW YORK CITY

The name of New York City, as it appears on all official documents, is *The City of New York*. This name applies to all five boroughs which consolidated in 1898 to form what is known as Greater New York. The five boroughs are Manhattan, The Bronx, Brooklyn, Queens, and Richmond. The term Greater New York is seldom used at the present time, and often the city is called New York City to distinguish it from New York State. The two Boroughs of Brooklyn and Queens are located on Long Island and the Borough of Richmond is located on Staten Island. The Borough of Manhattan is located on Manhattan Island, while The Bronx is located on the mainland of New York State. Because the city is large, covers much territory, and has so many people, the United States Post Office has divided the city for its own convenience; therefore, the post office address of people living in Manhattan is New York, New York. For those living in the Borough of Brooklyn, the post office address is Brooklyn, New York; and, likewise, each borough has its own special post office address.

18. New York City is referred to on all official documents as *Greater New York City.* 18._____

19. The boroughs of New York City were joined together in 1898 to make up Greater New York. 19._____

20. Greater New York is made up of five boroughs. 20._____

21. The boroughs which make up New York City are The Bronx, Richmond, Brooklyn, Queens, and Nassau. 21._____

22. The borough of Queens is located on the mainland of New York State. 22._____

23. The Bronx and Brooklyn are part of Long Island. 23._____

24. A letter for Manhattan should be addressed to New York, New York. 24._____

25. Because New York City is so big, the Post Office has divided it into five different post office addresses. 25._____

KEY (CORRECT ANSWERS)

1. A
2. B
3. D
4. F
5. F
6. T
7. F
8. T
9. F
10. T
11. F
12. F
13. T
14. T
15. F
16. T
17. F
18. F
19. T
20. T
21. F
22. F
23. F
24. T
25. T

TEST 2

Questions 1-4.

DIRECTIONS: Questions 1 through 4 are to be answered SOLELY on the basis of the following passage.

In the long run, a government will always encroach upon freedom to the extent which it has the power to do so; this is almost a natural law of politics since, whatever the intentions of the men who exercise political power, the sheer momentum of government leads to a constant pressure upon the liberties of the citizen. But in many countries, society has responded by throwing up its own defenses in the shape of social classes or organized corporations which, enjoying economic power and popular support, have been able to set limits to the scope of action of the executive. Such, for example, in England was the origin of all our liberties-won from government by the stand first of the feudal nobility, then of churches and political parties, and latterly of trade unions, commercial organizations, and the societies for promoting various causes. Even European lands which were arbitrarily ruled by the powers of the monarchy, though absolute in theory, were in their exercise checked in a similar fashion. Indeed, the fascist dictatorships of today are the first truly tyrannical governments which western Europe has known for centuries, and they have been rendered possible only because on coming to power they destroyed all forms of social organization which were in any way rivals to the state.

1. The MAIN idea of the above passage is BEST expressed as 1._____

   A. limited powers of monarchies
   B. the ideal of liberal government
   C. functions of trade unions
   D. ruthless ways of dictators

2. The writer maintains that there is a natural tendency for governments to 2._____

   A. become more democratic
   B. become fascist
   C. increase individual liberties
   D. assume more power

3. Monarchy was FIRST checked in England by the 3._____

   A. trade unions
   B. church
   C. people
   D. nobles

4. Fascist dictatorships differ from monarchies of recent times in 4._____

   A. getting things done by sheer momentum
   B. promoting various causes
   C. exerting constant pressure on liberties
   D. destroying people's organizations

Questions 5-8.

DIRECTIONS: Questions 5 through 8 are to be answered SOLELY on the basis of the following paragraph.

Very early on a summer's morning, the nicest thing to look at is a beach, before the swimmers arrive. Usually all the litter has been picked up from the sand by the Park Department clean-up crew. Everything is quiet. All you can hear are the waves breaking and the sea gulls calling to each other. The beach opens to the public at 10 A.M. Long before that time; however, long lines of eager men, women, and children have driven up to the entrance. They form long lines that wind around the beach waiting for the signal to move.

5. According to the above paragraph, before 10 A.M., long lines are formed that are made up of 5

   A. cars
   B. clean-up crews
   C. men, women, and children
   D. Park Department trucks

6. The season referred to in the above paragraph is 6

   A. fall
   B. summer
   C. winter
   D. spring

7. The place the above paragraph is describing is a 7

   A. beach
   B. Park
   C. golf course
   D. tennis court

8. According to the above paragraph, one of the things you notice early in the morning is that 8

   A. radios are playing
   B. swimmers are there
   C. the sand is dirty
   D. the litter is gone

Questions 9-10.

DIRECTIONS: Questions 9 and 10 are to be answered SOLELY on the basis of the following passage.

There have been almost as many definitions of *opinion* as there have been students of the problem, and the definitions have ranged from such a statement as *inconsistent views capable of being accepted by rational minds as true* to the *overt manifestation of an attitude.* There are, however, a number of clearly outstanding factors among the various definitions which form the sum total of the concept. Opinion is the stronghold of the individual. No *group* ever had an opinion, and there is no mechanism except that of the individual mind capable of forming an opinion. It is true, of course, that opinions can be altered or even created by the stimuli of environment. In the midst of individual diversity and confusion, every question as it rises into importance is subjected to a process of consolidation and clarification until there emerge certain views, each held and advocated in common by bodies of citizens. When a group of people accepts the same opinion, that opinion is public with respect to the group accepting it. When there is not unanimous opinion, there is not one public but two or more.

9. On the basis of the above passage, it may be INFERRED that 9.____

   A. all individual opinions are subjected to consolidation by the influence of environmental stimuli
   B. governments are influenced by opinions held in common by large groups of citizens
   C. some of the elements of the extremely varied definitions of *opinion* are compatible
   D. when there is no unanimity, there is no public opinion

10. On the basis of the above passage, the MOST accurate of the following statement is: 10.____

   A. One definition of *opinion* implies that most individuals can accept inconsistent views on the same question
   B. One other definition of *opinion* implies that the individual's attitude concerning a question must be openly expressed before it can be considered as an opinion
   C. The individual opinion plays no part in the stand taken on a given question by a group after the individual has identified himself with the group
   D. There are no group opinions formed on relatively unimportant issues because of individual confusion

Questions 11-13.

DIRECTIONS: Questions 11 through 13 are to be answered SOLELY on the basis of the following passage.

The word *propaganda* has fallen on evil days. As far as popular usage is concerned, its reputation by now is probably lost irretrievably, for its connotation is almost invariably sinister or evil. This is a pity for, in the struggle for men's minds, it is a weapon of great potential value. Indeed, in the race against time that we are running, its constructive use is indispensable. The student of propaganda must know that it is a term honorable in origin.

Propaganda is *good* or *bad* according to the virtue of the end to which it seeks to persuade us, and the methods it employs. Bad propaganda is distinguished by a disregard for the welfare of those at whom it is directed. Such disregard either derives from, or eventually results in, a lack of proper reverence for individuality, for the private person and our relation to him. For *man* is substituted mass, and the *mass* is manipulated for selfish purposes. The authoritarian reformist who believes he is acting *in the interest* of the masses is also involved in this same disregard for personal integrity. Its final outcome is always the same-a disregard for the individual. Good propaganda involves the deliberate avoidance of all casuistry. In so far as good propaganda operates upon us at a level of our weakness or disability, its intent must be to contribute a cure, not a sedative; inspiration, not an opiate; enlightenment, not accentuation of our ignorance.

11. Of the following, the MOST suitable title for the above passage is 11.____

   A. PROPAGANDA AND SOCIETY
   B. PROPAGANDA FOR THE MASSES
   C. THE PROPER MEANING OF PROPAGANDA
   D. SES AND MISUSES OF PROPAGANDA

12. On the basis of the above passage, it may be INFERRED that 12.

    A. some propaganda may employ unscrupulous methods to persuade us to ends that are justified
    B. the definition of the word *propaganda* has been changed
    C. the method of frequent repetition is an example of bad propaganda.
    D. the opportunity for the individual to challenge propaganda has decreased

13. On the basis of the above passage, it may be INFERRED that 13.

    A. a reformer who believes in his cause should not employ propaganda to advance it
    B. good propaganda should be limited to operating against the levels of weakness of the individual
    C. propaganda may lose sight of the welfare of the individual in its appeal to the masses
    D. those who have privileged access to the media of mass communication must always accept high standards in their use of propaganda

Questions 14-15.

DIRECTIONS: Questions 14 and 15 are to be answered SOLELY on the basis of the following passage.

A steadfast concert for peace can never be maintained except by a partnership of democratic nations. No autocratic government could be trusted to keep faith within it or observe its covenants. It must be a league of honor, a partnership of opinion. Intrigue would eat its vitals away; the plotting of inner circles who could plan what they would, and render account to no one, would be a corruption seated at its very heart. Only free people can hold their purpose and their honor steady to a common end, and prefer the interests of mankind to any narrow interest of their own.

14. According to the above paragraph, only democratic nations can 14

    A. be free of plotting, intrigue, and corruption
    B. be trusted to do what is right and honorable
    C. plan programs which promote the interests of their country
    D. subordinate their own interests to those which benefit the entire world

15. It may be implied from the above passage that an autocratic government could NOT be trusted to respect its international agreements because it 15

    A. exemplifies the proverb that there is no honor among thieves
    B. is full of corruption, plots, and intrigue
    C. is principally concerned with the welfare of its own people
    D. would plot with other governments to advance their own mutual interests

Questions 16-17.

DIRECTIONS: Questions 16 and 17 are to be answered SOLELY on the basis of the following passage.

A gentleman is mainly occupied in removing the obstacles which hinder the free and unembarrassed action of those about him; and he concurs with their movements rather than takes the initiative himself. The true gentleman carefully avoids whatever may cause a jar or jolt in the minds of those with whom he is cast. His great concern is to put everyone at his ease and to make all feel at home. He is tender towards the bashful, gentle towards the distant, and merciful towards the absurd; he can recollect to whom he is speaking; he guards against unseasonable allusions, or topics which may irritate; he is seldom prominent in conversation, and never wearisome.

16. According to the above passage, a gentleman makes it his business to 16.____

   A. discuss current issues of interest although controversial
   B. get the bashful to participate in the conversation
   C. introduce to one another guests who have not previously met
   D. remember the person with whom he is speaking

17. According to the above passage, one of the CHIEF characteristics of a gentleman is that he 17.____

   A. conducts himself in such a way as to avoid hurting the feelings of others
   B. keeps the conversation going, particularly when interest flags
   C. puts an unruly guest in his place politely but firmly
   D. shows his guests the ways in which they can best enjoy

18. Too often we retire people who are willing and able to continue working, according to Federal Security Agency Administrator Oscar R. Ewing in addressing the first National Conference on Aging; to point up the fact that chronological age is no longer an effective criterion in determining whether or not an individual is capable of working. The Second World War proved this point when it became necessary to hire older, experienced people to handle positions in business and industry vacated by personnel called to serve their country. As shown by production records set during the war period, the employment of older people helped us continue, and even better, our high level of production. 18.____
   It was also pointed out at the conference that our life expectancy is increasing and that the over-65 group will jump from 11,500,000 now to twenty million in 2015. A good many of these people are capable of producing and have a desire to work, but they are kept from gainful employment by a shortsightedness on the part of many employers which leads them to believe that young people alone can give them adequate service. It is true that the young person has greater agility and speed to offer, but on the other hand there is much to be gained from the experience, steadfastness, and maturity of judgment of the elderly worker.
   The title that BEST expresses the ideas of the above passage is

   A. INCREASED EFFICIENCY OF ELDERLY WORKERS
   B. MISJUDGING ELDERLY WORKERS
   C. LENGTHENING THE SPAN OF LIFE
   D. NEW JOBS FOR THE AGED

19. The question is whether night baseball will prove a boon or a disaster to the game. The big crowds now attending the night games, the brilliance of the spectacle, the miracle of the spinning turnstiles all these seem sufficient evidence that what is needed is not less night ball, but more. The fact remains, however, that despite all apparent success, some of the shrewdest, most experienced men in baseball remain unconvinced of the miracle. They are steady in their preference for daytime baseball, and they view with increasing distrust the race towards more lights. It could be that these men are simply being obstinate. Yet, on the other hand, it could be that in reviewing the caliber of baseball as it is played at night, in speculating upon the future effect of night ball, they are not entirely unprophetic. It could even be, indeed, that they are dead right. 19.

In his attitude toward the future of night baseball, the author expresses

A. uncertainty
B. confidence
C. optimism
D. sharp criticism

20. We all know people who would welcome a new American car to their stables, but one cannot expect to find a sports car man among them. He cannot be enticed into such a circus float without feeling soiled. He resents the wanton use of chromium as much as he shudders at the tail fins, the grotesquely convoluted bumpers, and other *dishonest* lines. He blanches at the enormous bustle that adds weight and useless space, drags on ramps and curbstones, and complicates the process of parking even in the car's own garage. The attitude of the owner of a Detroit product is reflected in the efforts of manufacturers to *take the drive out of driving.* The sports car addict regards this stand as outrageous. His interest in a car, he is forever telling himself and other captive listeners, lies in the fun of driving it, in *sensing its alertness on the road*, and in *pampering it as a thoroughbred.* 20.

The above passage implies that sports cars are very

A. colorful
B. showy
C. maneuverable
D. roomy

Questions 21-25.

DIRECTIONS: Questions 21 through 25 are to be answered SOLELY on the basis of the following passage.

Fuel is conserved when a boiler is operating near its most efficient load. The efficiency of a boiler will change as the output varies. Large amounts of air must be used at low ratings and so the heat exchanger is inefficient. As the output increases, the efficiency decreases due to an increase in flue gas temperature. Every boiler has an output rate for which its efficiency is highest. For example, in a water-tube boiler, the highest efficiency might occur at 120 percent of rated capacity while in a vertical fire-tube boiler highest efficiency might be at 70% of rated capacity. The type of fuel burned and cleanliness affects the maximum efficiency of the boiler. When a power plant contains a battery of boilers, a sufficient number should be kept in operation so as to maintain the output of individual units near their points of maximum efficiency. One of the boilers in the battery can be used as a regulator to meet the change in demand for steam while the other boilers could still operate at their most efficient rating. Boiler performance is expressed as the number of pounds of steam generated per pound of fuel.

21. According to the above paragraph, the number of pounds of steam generated per pound of fuel is a measure of boiler 21.____

A. size
B. performance
C. regulator input
D. bypass

22. According to the above paragraph, the HIGHEST efficiency of a vertical fire tube boiler might occur at _______ capacity. 22.____

A. 70% of rate
B. 80% of water tube
C. 95% of water tube
D. 120% of rated

23. According to the above paragraph, the MAXIMUM efficiency of a boiler is affected by 23.____

A. atmospheric temperature
B. atmospheric pressure
C. cleanliness
D. fire brick material

24. According to the above paragraph, a heat exchanger uses large amounts of air at low 24.____

A. fuel rates
B. ratings
C. temperatures
D. pressures

25. According to the above paragraph, one boiler in a battery of boilers should be used as a 25.____

A. demand
B. stand-by
C. regulator
D. safety

KEY (CORRECT ANSWERS)

1. D
2. D
3. D
4. D
5. C

6. B
7. A
8. D
9. C
10. B

11. D
12. A
13. C
14. D
15. D

16. D
17. A
18. B
19. A
20. C

21. B
22. A
23. C
24. B
25. C

TEST 3

Questions 1-7.

DIRECTIONS: Questions 1 through 7 are to be answered SOLELY on the basis of the following paragraph on FIRST AID INSTRUCTIONS.

FIRST AID INSTRUCTIONS

The main purpose of first aid is to put the injured person in the best possible position until medical help arrives. This includes the performance of emergency treatment designed to save a life if a doctor is not immediately available. When an accident happens, a crowd usually collects around the victim. If nobody uses his head, the injured person fails to receive the care he needs. You must keep calm and cool at all times and, most important, it is your duty to take charge at an accident. The first thing for you to do is to see, insofar as possible, what is wrong with the injured person. Leave him where he is until the nature and extent of his injury are determined. If he is unconscious, he should not be moved except to lay him flat on his back if he is in some other position. Loosen the clothing of any seriously hurt person, and make him as comfortable as possible. Medical help should be called as soon as possible. You should remain with the injured person and send someone else to call the doctor. You should try to make sure that the one who calls for a doctor is able to give correct information as to the location of the injured person. In order to help the physician to know what equipment may be needed in each particular case, the person making the call should give the doctor as much information about the injury as possible.

1. If nobody uses his head at the scene of an accident, there is danger that 1._

   A. a large crowd will gather
   B. emergency treatment will be needed
   C. names of witnesses will be missed
   D. the victim will not get the care he needs

2. The FIRST thing you should do at the scene of an accident is to 2._

   A. call a doctor
   B. lay the injured person on his back
   C. find out what is wrong with the injured person
   D. loosen the clothing of the injured person

3. Until the nature and extent of the injuries are determined you should 3._

   A. move the injured person indoors
   B. let the injured person lie where he is
   C. carefully roll the injured person on his back
   D. give the injured person artificial respiration

4. If the injured person is unconscious, you should 4._

   A. give him artificial respiration
   B. get some hot liquid like coffee into him
   C. lay him flat on his back
   D. move him to a comfortable location

5. If a doctor is to be called, you should 5.____

   A. go make this call yourself since you have all the information
   B. go make this call yourself since you are in charge
   C. send someone who knows what happened
   D. send someone who is fast

6. The person calling the doctor should give as much information as he has regarding the injury so that the doctor 6.____

   A. can bring the necessary equipment
   B. can decide whether he should come
   C. will know whom to notify
   D. can advise what should be done

7. The MAIN purpose of first aid is to 7.____

   A. stop bleeding
   B. prevent further complications of the injury
   C. keep the patient comfortable
   D. determine what the injuries are

Questions 8-13.

DIRECTIONS: Questions 8 through 13 are to be answered SOLELY on the basis of the following passage regarding selection of tours of duty.

SELECTION OF TOURS OF DUTY

A selection of tours of duty for the winter season for Railroad Porters will begin on Monday, December 27, and conclude on Thursday, December 30.

The selection will take place in Room 828, 8th Floor, 370 Jay Street, Telephone Elmer 2-5000, Extension 3870.

Railroad Porters whose names appear on the attached schedule will make selections at the time and date indicated.

8. The selection of tours of duty began on 8.____

   A. Monday
   B. Tuesday
   C. Wednesday
   D. Thursday

9. No selections of tours of duty were scheduled for December 9.____

   A. 28
   B. 29
   C. 30
   D. 31

10. The choice of tours of duty was PROBABLY based on 10.____

   A. age
   B. seniority
   C. borough of residence
   D. alphabetical listing of names

11. The season for which the selection of tours of duty was made was the 11.___

A. spring
B. summer
C. autumn
D. winter

12. A porter making a selection had to do so 12.___

A. before work
B. after work
C. on his day off
D. at the time indicated

13. The selecting was to be done by 13.___

A. all station employees
B. all porters
C. only the porters whose names were on the schedule
D. employees not satisfied with present schedules

Questions 14-16.

DIRECTIONS: Questions 14 through 16 are to be answered SOLELY on the basis of the following passage concerning car inspection and cleaning information.

RIGID INSPECTION: Subway cars are hauled into a repair yard and given a rigid inspection about three times a month.

SWEEPING AND WASHING: Each car is swept every twenty-four hours. Its Windows are washed every time it comes into a repair yard.

OVERHAUL: At the completion of 90,000 miles, the car is almost completely taken apart, cleaned, and painted.

14. Car windows are USUALLY washed at least once in 14.___

A. one day
B. three days
C. ten days
D. three months

15. If the average car traveled about 75,000 miles per year, it would NORMALLY be almost completely taken apart, cleaned, and painted about every 15.___

A. 9 months
B. year
C. 15 months
D. 2 years

16. If a car has been overhauled at the end of 90,000 miles, it would be brought back to the repair yard 16.___

A. within one week for sweeping
B. within two weeks for another overhaul
C. after 90,000 miles for inspection if necessary
D. within two weeks for a rigid inspection

Questions 17-19.

DIRECTIONS: Questions 17 through 19 are to be answered SOLELY on the basis of the following passage.

Into the nine square miles that make up Manhattan's business districts, about two million people travel each weekday to go to work-the equivalent of the combined populations of Boston, Baltimore, and Cincinnati. Some 140,000 drive there in cars, 200,000 take buses, and 100,000 ride the commuter railroads. The great majority, however, go by subway approximately 1.4 million people.

It is some ride. The last major improvement in the subway system was completed in 1935. The subways are dirty and noisy. Many local lines operate well beneath capacity, but many express lines are strained way beyond capacity–in particular, the lines to Manhattan, now overloaded by 39,000 passengers during peak hours.

But for all its discomforts, the subway system is inherently a far more efficient way of moving people than automobiles and highways. Making this system faster, more convenient, and more comfortable for people must be the core of the City's transportation effort.

17. The CENTRAL point of the above passage is that 17._____

A. the equivalent of the combined populations of Boston, Baltimore, and Cincinnati commute into Manhattan's business district each weekday
B. the improvement of the subway system is the key to the solution of moving people efficiently in and out of Manhattan's business district
C. the subways are dirty and noisy, resulting in a terrible ride
D. we should increase the ability of people to get in and out of Manhattan by cars, subways, and commuter railroads in order to ease the load from the subways.

18. In accordance with the above passage, 1.4 million people commute by subway and _______ by other mass transportation means. 18._____

A. 200,000
B. 100,000
C. 440,000
D. 300,000

19. From the information given in the above passage, one could logically conclude that, next to the subways, the transportation system that carries the LARGEST number of passengers is 19._____

A. railroads
B. cars
C. buses
D. local lines

Questions 20-25.

DIRECTIONS: Questions 20 through 25 are to be answered SOLELY on the basis of the following passage. Each question consists of a statement. You are to indicate whether the statement is TRUE (T) or FALSE (F).

THE CITY

The City, which at one time in 1789-90 was the capital of the nation and which was also the capital of the State until 1796, has continued as the financial and economic capital of the United States and has grown to be the greatest city in the country.

The City is great because it has such a large population-a total of eight million persons in 2008. This population is larger than the total inhabitants of 41 of 75 of the largest countries in the world. The City requires many homes and buildings to accommodate its residents. The City consists of more than 725,000 buildings, more than half of which are one and two family houses owned by the occupants. More than five hundred hotels, with 128,000 rooms, are needed to take care of the visitors to the City; it is estimated that between one and two hundred thousand people visit the City daily.

The harbor is so large that any six of the other leading seaports of the world could be placed in it. Its piers, to accommodate freight and passengers, number 471, and its waterfront covers 770 miles.

20. The City has been the capital of the United States and also the capital of the State. 20.

21. In 1988, the population of the City was greater than the total population of forty-one of seventy-five of the largest countries in the world. 21.

22. Over half of all the buildings in the City are one and two family homes which are owned by the people who live in them? 22.

23. A little under 200,000 people visit the City each year. 23.

24. The harbor is larger than any other leading seaport. 24.

25. The harbor is 471 miles long and has 770 piers to take care of passengers and cargo. 25

KEY (CORRECT ANSWERS)

1. D
2. C
3. B
4. C
5. C
6. A
7. B
8. A
9. D
10. B
11. D
12. D
13. C
14. C
15. C
16. D
17. B
18. D
19. C
20. T
21. T
22. T
23. F
24. T
25. F

READING COMPREHENSION
UNDERSTANDING AND INTERPRETING WRITTEN MATERIAL
EXAMINATION SECTION
TEST 1

DIRECTIONS: Each question or incomplete statement is followed by several suggested answers or completions. Select the one that BEST answers the question or completes the statement. *PRINT THE LETTER OF THE CORRECT ANSWER IN THE SPACE AT THE RIGHT.*

Questions 1-4.

DIRECTIONS: Questions 1 through 4 are to be answered SOLELY on the basis of the following paragraph.

An annual leave allowance, which combines leaves previously given for vacation, personal business, family illness, and other reasons shall be granted members. Calculation of credits for such leave shall be on an annual basis beginning January 1st of each year. Annual leave credits shall be based on time served by members during preceding calendar year. However, when credits have been accrued and member retires during current year, additional annual leave credits shall, in this instance, be granted at accrual rate of three days for each completed month of service, excluding terminal leave. If accruals granted for completed months of service extend into following month, member shall be granted an additional three days accrual for completed month. This shall be the only condition where accruals in a current year are granted for vacation period in such year.

1. According to the above paragraph, if a fireman's wife were to become seriously ill so that he would take time off from work to be with her, such time off would be deducted from his _______ allowance. 1.____

   A. annual leave
   B. vacation leave
   C. personal business leave
   D. family illness leave

2. Terminal leave means leave taken 2.____

   A. at the end of the calendar year
   B. at the end of the vacation year
   C. immediately before retirement
   D. before actually earned, because of an emergency

3. A fireman appointed on July 1, 2007 will be able to take his first full or normal annual leave during the period 3.____

   A. July 1, 2007 to June 30, 2008
   B. Jan. 1, 2008 to Dec. 31, 2008
   C. July 1, 2008 to June 30, 2009
   D. Jan. 1, 2009 to Dec. 31, 2009

4. According to the above paragraph, a member who retires on July 15 of this year will be entitled to receive leave allowance based on this year of _______ days. 4._

   A. 15 B. 18 C. 22 D. 24

5. Fire alarm boxes are electromechanical devices for transmitting a coded signal. In each box, there is a trainwork of wheels. When the box is operated, a spring-activated code wheel within begins to revolve. The code number of the box is notched on the circumference of the code wheel, and the latter is associated with the circuit in such a way that when it revolves it causes the circuit to open and close in a predetermined manner, thereby transmitting its particular signal to the central station. A fire alarm box is nothing more than a device for interrupting the flow of current in a circuit in such a way as to produce a coded signal that may be decoded by the dispatchers in the central office. 5._
   Based on the above, select the FALSE statement:

   A. Each standard fire alarm box has its own code wheel
   B. The code wheel operates when the box is pulled
   C. The code wheel is operated electrically
   D. Only the break in the circuit by the notched wheel causes the alarm signal to be transmitted to the central office

Questions 6-9.

DIRECTIONS: Questions 6 through 9 are to be answered SOLELY on the basis of the following paragraph.

Ventilation, as used in fire fighting operations, means opening up a building or structure in which a fire is burning to release the accumulated heat, smoke, and gases. Lack of knowledge of the principles of ventilation on the part of firemen may result in unnecessary punishment due to ventilation being neglected or improperly handled. While ventilation itself extinguishes no fires, when used in an intelligent manner, it allows firemen to get at the fire more quickly, easily, and with less danger and hardship.

6. According to the above paragraph, the MOST important result of failure to apply the principles of ventilation at a fire may be 6._

   A. loss of public confidence
   B. waste of water
   C. excessive use of equipment
   D. injury to firemen

7. It may be inferred from the above paragraph that the CHIEF advantage of ventilation is that it 7._

   A. eliminates the need for gas masks
   B. reduces smoke damage
   C. permits firemen to work closer to the fire
   D. cools the fire

8. Knowledge of the principles of ventilation, as defined in the above paragraph, would be LEAST important in a fire in a 8._____

   A. tenement house
   B. grocery store
   C. ship's hold
   D. lumberyard

9. We may conclude from the above paragraph that for the well-trained and equipped fireman, ventilation is 9._____

   A. a simple matter
   B. rarely necessary
   C. relatively unimportant
   D. a basic tool

Questions 10-13.

DIRECTIONS: Questions 10 through 13 are to be answered SOLELY on the basis of the following passage.

Fire exit drills should be established and held periodically to effectively train personnel to leave their working area promptly upon proper signal and to evacuate the building, speedily but without confusion. All fire exit drills should be carefully planned and carried out in a serious manner under rigid discipline so as to provide positive protection in the event of a real emergency. As a general rule, the local fire department should be furnished advance information regarding the exact date and time the exit drill is scheduled. When it is impossible to hold regular drills, written instructions should be distributed to all employees.

Depending upon individual circumstances, fires in warehouses vary from those of fast development that are almost instantly beyond any possibility of employee control to others of relatively slow development where a small readily attackable flame may be present for periods of time up to 15 minutes or more during which simple attack with fire extinguishers or small building hoses may prevent the fire development. In any case, it is characteristic of many warehouse fires that at a certain point in development they flash up to the top of the stack, increase heat quickly, and spread rapidly. There is a degree of inherent danger in attacking warehouse type fires, and all employees should be thoroughly trained in the use of the types of extinguishers or small hoses in the buildings and well instructed in the necessity of always staying between the fire and a direct pass to an exit.

10. Employees should be instructed that, when fighting a fire, they MUST 10._____

    A. try to control the blaze
    B. extinguish any fire in 15 minutes
    C. remain between the fire and a direct passage to the exit
    D. keep the fire between themselves and the fire exit

11. Whenever conditions are such that regular fire drills cannot be held, then which one of the following actions should be taken? 11._____

    A. The local fire department should be notified.
    B. Rigid discipline should be maintained during work hours.
    C. Personnel should be instructed to leave their working area by whatever means are available.
    D. Employees should receive fire drill procedures in writing.

12. The above passage indicates that the purpose of fire exit drills is to train employees to 12._

    A. control a fire before it becomes uncontrollable
    B. act as firefighters
    C. leave the working area promptly
    D. be serious

13. According to the above passage, fire exit drills will prove to be of UTMOST effectiveness if 13._

    A. employee participation is made voluntary
    B. they take place periodically
    C. the fire department actively participates
    D. they are held without advance planning

Questions 14-16.

DIRECTIONS: Questions 14 through 16 are to be answered SOLELY on the basis of the following paragraph.

The heat output from unit heaters will depend on how fast and how completely dry hot steam fills the unit core. For complete and fast air removal and rapid drainage of condensate, use a trap actuated by water or vapor (inverted bucket trap) and not a trap operated by temperature only (thermostatic or bellows trap). A temperature-actuated trap will hold back the hot condensate until it cools to a point where the thermal element opens. When this happens, the condensate backs up in the heater and reduces the heat output. With a water-actuated trap, this will not happen as the water or condensate is discharged as fast as it is formed.

14. On the basis of the information given in the above paragraph, it can be concluded that the PROPER type of trap to use for a unit heater is a(n) _______ trap. 14._

    A. thermostatic
    B. bellows-type
    C. inverted bucket
    D. temperature

15. According to the above paragraph, the MAIN reason for using the type of trap specified for a unit heater is to 15._

    A. bring the condensate up to steam temperature
    B. prevent reduction in the heat output of the unit heater
    C. permit cycling of the heater
    D. maintain constant temperature of condensate in the trap

16. As used in the above paragraph, the word *actuated* means MOST NEARLY 16._

    A. clogged
    B. operated
    C. cleaned
    D. vented

Question 17 -25.

DIRECTIONS: Questions 17 through 25 are to be answered SOLELY on the basis of the following passage. Each question consists of a statement. You are to indicate whether the statement is TRUE (T) or FALSE (F).

MOVING AN OFFICE

An office with all its equipment is sometimes moved during working hours. This is a difficult task and must be done in an orderly manner to avoid confusion. The operation should be planned in such a way as not to interrupt the progress of work usually done in the office and to make possible the accurate placement of the furniture and records in the new location. If the office moves to a place inside the same building, the desks and files are moved with all their contents. If the movement is to another building, the contents of each desk and file are placed in boxes. Each box is marked with a letter showing the particular section in the new quarters to which it is to be moved. Also marked on each box is the number of the desk or file on which the box is to be placed. Each piece of equipment must have a numbered tag. The number of each piece of equipment is put in soft chalk on the floor in the new office to show the proper location, and several floor plans are made to show where each piece of equipment goes. When the moving is done, someone is stationed at each of the several exits of the old office to see that each box or piece of equipment has its destination clearly marked on it. At the new office, someone stands at each of the several entrances with a copy of the floor plan and directs the placing of the furniture and equipment according to the floor plan. No one should interfere at this point with the arrangements shown on the plan. Improvements in arrangement can be considered and made at a later date.

17. It is a hard job to move an office from one place to another during working hours. 17.____

18. Confusion cannot be avoided if an office is moved during working hours. 18.____

19. The work usually done in an office must be stopped for the day when the office is moved during working hours. 19.____

20. If an office is moved from one floor to another in the same building, the contents of a desk are taken out and put into boxes for moving. 20.____

21. If boxes are used to hold material from desks when moving an office, the box is numbered the same as the desk on which it is to be put. 21.____

22. Letters are marked in soft chalk on the floor at the new quarters to show where the desks should go when moved. 22.____

23. When the moving begins, a person is put at each exit of the old office to check that each box and piece of equipment has clearly marked on it where it to go. 23.____

24. A person stationed at each entrance of the new quarters to direct the placing of the furniture and equipment has a copy of the floor plan of the new quarters. 24.____

25. If, while the furniture is being moved into the new office, a person helping at a doorway gets an idea of a better way to arrange the furniture, he should change the planned arrangement and make a record of the change. 25.____

KEY (CORRECT ANSWERS)

1.	A	11.	D
2.	C	12.	C
3.	D	13.	B
4.	B	14.	C
5.	C	15.	B
6.	D	16.	B
7.	C	17.	T
8.	D	18.	F
9.	D	19.	F
10.	C	20.	F

21. T
22. F
23. T
24. T
25. F

TEST 2

Questions 1-4.

DIRECTIONS: Questions 1 through 4 are to be answered SOLELY on the basis of the following paragraph.

In all cases of homicide, members of the Police Department who investigate will make every effort to obtain statements from dying persons. Such statements are of the greatest importance to the District Attorney. In many cases, there may be a failure to solve the crime if they are not taken. The principal element to be considered in taking the declaration of a dying person is his mental attitude. In order to be admissible in evidence, the person must have no hope of recovery. The patient will be fully interrogated on that point before a statement is taken.

1. In cases of homicide, according to the above paragraph, members of the police force will 1.____

   A. try to change the mental attitude of the dying person
   B. attempt to obtain a statement from the dying person
   C. not give the information they obtain directly to the District Attorney
   D. be careful not to injure the dying person unnecessarily

2. The mental attitude of the person making the dying statement is of GREAT importance because it can determine, according to the above paragraph, whether the 2.____

   A. victim should be interrogated in the presence of witnesses
   B. victim will be willing to make a statement of any kind
   C. statement will tell the District Attorney who committed the crime
   D. the statement can be used as evidence

3. District Attorneys find that statements of a dying person are important, according to the above paragraph, because 3.____

   A. it may be that the victim will recover and then refuse to testify
   B. they are important elements in determining the mental attitude of the victim
   C. they present a point of view
   D. it may be impossible to punish the criminal without such a statement

4. A well-known gangster is found dying from a bullet wound. The patrolman first on the scene, in the presence of witnesses, tells the man that he is going to die and asks, *Who shot you?* The gangster says, *Jones shot me, but he hasn't killed me. I'll live to get him.* He then falls back dead. According to the above paragraph, this statement is 4.____

   A. *admissible* in evidence; the man was obviously speaking the truth
   B. *not admissible* in evidence; the man obviously did not believe that he was dying
   C. *admissible* in evidence; there were witnesses to the statement
   D. *not admissible* in evidence; the victim did not sign any statement and the evidence is merely hearsay

Questions 5-7.

DIRECTIONS: Questions 5 through 7 are to be answered SOLELY on the basis of the following paragraph.

The factors contributing to crime and delinquency are varied and complex. The home and its immediate environment have been found to be crucial in determining the behavior patterns of the individual, and criminality can frequently be traced to faulty family relationships and a bad neighborhood. But in the search for a clearer understanding of the underlying causes of delinquent and criminal behavior, the total environment must be taken into consideration.

5. According to the above paragraph, family relationships 5._

   A. tend to become faulty in bad neighborhoods
   B. are important in determining the actions of honest people as well as criminals
   C. are the only important element in the understanding of causes of delinquency
   D. are determined by the total environment

6. According to the above paragraph, the causes of crime and delinquency are 6._

   A. not simple
   B. not meaningless
   C. meaningless
   D. simple

7. According to the above paragraph, faulty family relationships FREQUENTLY are 7._

   A. responsible for varied and complex results
   B. caused when one or both parents have a criminal behavior pattern
   C. independent of the total environment
   D. the cause of criminal acts

Questions 8-10.

DIRECTIONS: Questions 8 through 10 are to be answered SOLELY on the basis of the following paragraph.

A change in the specific problems which confront the police and in the methods for dealing with them has taken place in the last few decades. The automobile is a two-way symbol of this change in policing. It menaces every city with a complicated traffic problem and has speeded up the process of committing a crime and making a getaway, but at the same time has increased the effectiveness of police operations. However, the major concern of police departments continues to be the antisocial or criminal actions and behavior of human beings.

8. On the basis of the above paragraph, it can be stated that, for the most part, in the past few decades the specific problems of a police force 8._

   A. have changed but the general problems have not
   B. as well as the general problems have changed
   C. have remained the same but the general problems have changed
   D. as well as the general problems have remained the same

9. According to the above paragraph, advances in science and industry have, in general, made the police 9._

   A. operations less effective from the overall point of view
   B. operations more effective from the overall point of view
   C. abandon older methods of solving police problems
   D. concern themselves more with the antisocial acts of human beings

10. The automobile is a *two-way symbol,* according to the above paragraph, because its use 10.____

    A. has speeded up getting to and away from the scene of a crime
    B. both helps and hurts police operations
    C. introduces a new antisocial act—traffic violation—and does away with criminals like horse thieves
    D. both increases and decreases speed by introducing traffic problems

Questions 11-14.

DIRECTIONS: Questions 11 through 14 are to be answered SOLELY on the basis of the following passage on INSTRUCTIONS TO COIN AND TOKEN CASHIERS.

INSTRUCTIONS TO COIN AND TOKEN CASHIERS

Cashiers should reset the machine registers to an even starting number before commencing the day's work. Money bags received directly from collecting agents shall be counted and receipted for on the collecting agent's form. Each cashier shall be responsible for all coin or token bags accepted by him. He must examine all bags to be used for bank deposits for cuts and holes before placing them in use. Care must be exercised so that bags are not cut in opening them. Each bag must be opened separately and verified before another bag is opened. The machine register must be cleared before starting the count of another bag. The amount shown on the machine register must be compared with the amount on the bag tag. The empty bag must be kept on the table for re-examination should there be a difference between the amount on the bag tag and the amount on the machine register.

11. A cashier should BEGIN his day's assignment by 11.____

    A. counting and accepting all money bags
    B. resetting the counting machine register
    C. examining all bags for cuts and holes
    D. verifying the contents of all money bags

12. In verifying the amount of money in the bags received from the collecting agent, it is BEST to 12.____

    A. check the amount in one bag at a time
    B. base the total on the amount on the collecting agent's form
    C. repeat the total shown on the bag tag
    D. refer to the bank deposit receipt

13. A cashier is instructed to keep each empty coin bag on. his table while verifying its contents CHIEFLY because, long as the bag is on the table, 13.____

    A. it cannot be misplaced
    B. the supervisor can see how quickly the cashier works
    C. cuts and holes are easily noticed
    D. a recheck is possible in case the machine count disagrees with the bag tag total

14. The INSTRUCTIONS indicate that it is NOT proper procedure for a cashier to 14._

A. assume that coin bags are free of cuts and holes
B. compare the machine register total with the total shown on the bag tag
C. sign a form when he receives coin bags
D. reset the machine register before starting the day's counting

Questions 15-17.

DIRECTIONS: Questions 15 through 17 are to be answered SOLELY on the basis of the following passage.

The mass media are an integral part of the daily life of virtually every American. Among these media the youngest, television, is the most pervasive. Ninety-five percent of American homes have at least one T.V. set, and on the average that set is in use for about 40 hours each week. The central place of television in American life makes this medium the focal point of a growing national concern over the effects of media portrayals of violence on the values, attitudes, and behavior of an ever increasing audience.

In our concern about violence and its causes, it is easy to make television a scapegoat. But we emphasize the fact that there is no simple answer to the problem of violence – no single explanation of its causes, and no single prescription for its control. It should be remembered that America also experienced high levels of crime and violence in periods before the advent of television.

The problem of balance, taste, and artistic merit in entertaining programs on television are complex. We cannot countenance government censorship of television. Nor would we seek to impose arbitrary limitations on programming which might jeopardize television's ability to deal in dramatic presentations with controversial social issues. Nonetheless, we are deeply troubled by television's constant portrayal of violence, not in any genuine attempt to focus artistic expression on the human condition, but rather in pandering to a public preoccupation with violence that television itself has helped to generate.

15. According to the above passage, television uses violence MAINLY 15._

A. to highlight the reality of everyday existence
B. to satisfy the audience's hunger for destructive action
C. to shape the values and attitudes of the public
D. when it films documentaries concerning human conflict

16. Which one of the following statements is BEST supported by the above passage? 16._

A. Early American history reveals a crime pattern which is not related to television.
B. Programs should give presentations of social issues and never portray violent acts.
C. Television has proven that entertainment programs can easily make the balance between taste and artistic merit a simple matter.
D. Values and behavior should be regulated by governmental censorship.

17. Of the following, which word has the same meaning as *countenance*, as used in the above passage? 17._

A. Approve B. Exhibit C. Oppose D. Reject

DIRECTIONS: Questions 18 through 21 are to be answered SOLELY on the basis of the following passage.

Maintenance of leased or licensed areas on public parks or lands has always been a problem. A good rule to follow in the administration and maintenance of such areas is to limit the responsibility of any lessee or licensee to the maintenance of the structures and grounds essential to the efficient operation of the concession, not including areas for the general use of the public, such as picnic areas, public comfort stations, etc.; except where such facilities are leased to another public agency or where special conditions make such inclusion practicable, and where a good standard of maintenance can be assured and enforced. If local conditions and requirements are such that public use areas are included, adequate safeguards to the public should be written into contracts and enforced in their administration, to insure that maintenance by the concessionaire shall be equal to the maintenance standards for other park property.

18. According to the above passage, when an area on a public park is leased to a concessionaire, it is usually BEST to 18.____

A. confine the responsibility of the concessionaire to operation of the facilities and leave the maintenance function to the park agency
B. exclude areas of general public use from the maintenance obligation of the concessionaire
C. make the concessionaire responsible for maintenance of the entire area including areas of general public use
D. provide additional comfort station facilities for the area

19. According to the above passage, a valid reason for giving a concessionaire responsibility for maintenance of a picnic area within his leased area is that 19.____

A. local conditions and requirements make it practicable
B. more than half of the picnic area falls within his leased area
C. the concessionaire has leased picnic facilities to another public agency
D. the picnic area falls entirely within his leased area

20. According to the above passage, a precaution that should be taken when a concessionaire is made responsible for maintenance of an area of general public use in a park is 20.____

A. making sure that another public agency has not previously been made responsible for this area
B. providing the concessionaire with up-to-date equipment, if practicable
C. requiring that the concessionaire take out adequate insurance for the protection of the public
D. writing safeguards to the public into the contract

KEY (CORRECT ANSWERS)

1.	B	11.	B
2.	D	12.	A
3.	D	13.	D
4.	B	14.	A
5.	B	15.	B
6.	A	16.	A
7.	D	17.	A
8.	A	18.	B
9.	B	19.	A
10.	B	20.	D

TEST 3

Questions 1-5.

DIRECTIONS: Questions 1 through 5 are to be answered SOLELY on the basis of the following paragraph.

Physical inspections are an important tool for the examiner because he will have to decide the case in many instances on the basis of the inspection report. Most proceedings in a rent office are commenced by the filing of a written application or complaint by an interested party; that is, either the landlord or the tenant. Such an application or complaint must be filed in duplicate in order that the opposing party may be served with a copy of the application or complaint and thus be given an opportunity to answer and oppose it. Sometimes, a further opportunity is given the applicant to file a written rebuttal or reply to his adversary's answer. Often an examiner can make a determination or decision based on the written application, the answer, and the reply to the answer; and, of course, it would speed up operations if it were always possible to make decisions based on written documents only. Unfortunately, decisions can't always be made that way. There are numerous occasions where disputed issues of fact remain which cannot be resolved on the basis of the written statements of the parties. Typical examples are the following: The tenant claims that the refrigerator or stove or bathroom fixture is not functioning properly and the landlord denies this. It is obvious that in such cases an inspection of the accommodations is almost the only means of resolving such disputed issues.

1. According to the above paragraph, 1._____

   A. physical inspections are made in all cases
   B. physical inspections are seldom made
   C. it is sometimes possible to determine the facts in a case without a physical inspection
   D. physical inspections are made when it is necessary to verify the examiner's determination

2. According to the above paragraph, in MOST cases, proceedings are started by a(n) 2._____

   A. inspector discovering a violation
   B. oral complaint by a tenant or landlord
   C. request from another agency, such as the Building Department
   D. written complaint by a tenant or landlord

3. According to the above paragraph, when a tenant files an application with the rent office, the landlord is 3._____

   A. not told about the proceeding until after the examiner makes his determination
   B. given the duplicate copy of the application
   C. notified by means of an inspector visiting the premises
   D. not told about the proceeding until after the inspector has visited the Premises

4. As used in the above paragraph, the word *disputed* means MOST NEARLY 4._____

   A. unsettled
   B. contested
   C. definite
   D. difficult

5. As used in the above paragraph, the word *resolved* means MOST NEARLY 5.

A. settled B. fixed C. helped D. amended

Questions 6-10.

DIRECTIONS: Questions 6 through 10 are to be answered SOLELY on the basis of the following paragraph.

The examiner should order or request an inspection of the housing accommodations. His request for a physical inspection should be in writing, identify the accommodations and the landlord and the tenant, and specify precisely just what the inspector is to look for and report on. Unless this request is specific and lists in detail every item which the examiner wishes to be reported, the examiner will find that the inspection has not served its purpose and that even with the inspector's report, he is still in no position to decide the case due to loose ends which have not been completely tied up. The items that the examiner is interested in should be separately numbered on the inspection request and the same number referred to in the inspector's report. You can see what it would mean if an inspector came back with a report that did not cover everything. It may mean a tremendous waste of time and often require a re-inspection.

6. According to the above paragraph, the inspector makes an inspection on the order of 6._

A. the landlord
B. the tenant
C. the examiner
D. both the landlord and the tenant

7. According to the above paragraph, the reason for numbering each item that an inspector reports on is so that 7._

A. the report is neat
B. the report can be easily read and referred to
C. none of the examiner's requests for information is missed
D. the report will be specific

8. The one of the following items that is NOT necessarily included in the request for inspection is 8._

A. location of dwelling
B. name of landlord
C. item to be checked
D. type of building

9. As used in the above paragraph, the word precisely means MOST NEARLY 9._

A. exactly B. generally C. Usually D. strongly

10. As used in the above paragraph, the words in detail mean MOST NEARLY 10._

A. clearly
B. item by item
C. substantially
D. completely

Questions 11-13.

DIRECTIONS: Questions 11 through 13 are to be answered SOLELY on the basis of the following passage.

The agreement under which a tenant rents property from a landlord is known as a lease. Generally speaking, leases are classified as either short-term or long-term in duration. They are further subdivided according to the method used to determine the amount of periodic rent payments. Of the following types of lease in use, the more commonly used ones are the following:

1. The straight or fixed lease is one in which rent may be paid in equal amounts throughout the duration of the lease. These are usually restricted to short-term leasing, or somewhat longer-term if clauses in the lease provide for periodic escalation of payments as the economy shifts.
2. Percentage leasing, used for short-term commercial leasing, provides the landlord with a stipulated percentage of a tenant's gross sales from goods and services sold on the premises, in addition to a fixed amount of rent.
3. The net lease, generally long-term (ten years or more), requires the tenant to pay all operating costs, including real estate taxes and insurance. In a net-net lease, the tenant further agrees to meet mortgage interest and principal payments.
4. An escalated lease, which is a long-term lease, requires rent to be of a stipulated base amount which periodically is subject to escalation in accordance with cost-of-living index scales, or in direct proportion to taxes, insurance, and operating costs.

11. Based on the information given in the passage, which type of lease is MOST likely to be advantageous to a landlord if there is a high rate of inflation? _______ lease. 11._____

A. Fixed B. Percentage C. Net D. Escalated

12. On the basis of the above passage, which types of lease would generally be MOST suitable for a well-established textile company which requires permanent facilities for its large operations? 12._____
_______ lease and _______ lease.

A. Percentage; escalated
B. Escalated; net
C. Straight; net
D. Straight; percentage

13. According to the above passage, the ONLY type of lease which assures the same amount of rent throughout a specified interval is the _______ lease. 13._____

A. straight B. percentage C. net-net D. escalated

Questions 14-15.

DIRECTIONS: Questions 14 and 15 are to be answered SOLELY on the basis of the following passage.

If you like people, if you seek contact with them rather than hide yourself in a corner, if you study your fellow men sympathetically, if you try consistently to contribute something to their success and happiness, if you are reasonably generous with your thought and your time, if you have a partial reserve with everyone but a seeming reserve with no one, you will get along with your superiors, your subordinates, and the human race.

By the scores of thousands, precepts and platitudes have been written for the guidance of personal conduct. The odd part of it is that, despite all of this labor, most of the frictions in modern society arise from the individual's feeling of inferiority, his false pride, his vanity, his unwillingness to yield space to any other man and his consequent urge to throw his own weight around. Goethe said that the quality which best enables a man to renew his own life, in his relation to others, is his capability of renouncing particular things at the right moment in order warmly to embrace something new in the next.

14. On the basis of the above passage, it may be INFERRED that 14._

   A. a person should be unwilling to renounce privileges
   B. a person should realize that loss of a desirable job assignment may come at an opportune moment
   C. it is advisable for a person to maintain a considerable amount of reserve in his relationship with unfamiliar people
   D. people should be ready to contribute generously to a worthy charity

15. Of the following, the MOST valid implication made by the above passage is that 15._

   A. a wealthy person who spends a considerable amount of money entertaining his friends is not really getting along with them
   B. if a person studies his fellow men carefully and impartially, he will tend to have good relationships with them
   C. individuals who maintain seemingly little reserve in their relationships with people have in some measure overcome their own feelings of inferiority
   D. most precepts that have been written for the guidance of personal conduct in relationships with other people are invalid

Questions 16-17.

DIRECTIONS: Questions 16 and 17 are to be answered SOLELY on the basis of the following passage.

When a design for a new bank note of the Federal Government has been prepared by the Bureau of Engraving and Printing and has been approved by the Secretary of the Treasury, the engravers begin the work of cutting the design in steel. No one engraver does all the work. Each man is a specialist. One works only on portraits, another on lettering, another on scroll work, and so on. Each engraver, with a steel tool known as a graver, and aided by a powerful magnifying glass, carefully carves his portion of the design into the steel. He knows that one false cut or a slip of his tool, or one miscalculation of width or depth of line, may destroy the merit of his work. A single mistake means that months or weeks of labor will have been in vain. The Bureau is proud of the fact that no counterfeiter ever has duplicated the excellent work of its expert engravers.

16. According to the above passage, each engraver in the Bureau of Engraving and Printing 16._

   A. must be approved by the Secretary of the Treasury before he can begin work on the design for a new bank note
   B. is responsible for engraving a complete design of a new bank note by himself
   C. designs new bank notes and submits them for approval to the Secretary of the Treasury
   D. performs only a specific part of the work of engraving a design for a new bank note

17. According to the above passage, 17._____

A. an engraver's tools are not available to a counterfeiter
B. mistakes made in engraving a design can be corrected immediately with little delay in the work of the Bureau
C. the skilled work of the engravers has not been successfully reproduced by counterfeiter
D. careful carving and cutting by the engravers is essential to prevent damage to equipment

Questions 18-21.

DIRECTIONS: Questions 18 through 21 are to be answered SOLELY on the basis of the following passage.

In the late fifties, the average American housewife spent $4.50 per day for a family of four on food and 5.15 hours in food preparation, if all of her food was *home prepared;* she spent $5.80 per day and 3.25 hours if all of her food was purchased *partially prepared;* and $6.70 per day and 1.65 hours if all of her food was purchased *ready to serve.*

Americans spent about 20 billion dollars for food products in 1941. They spent nearly 70 billion dollars in 1958. They spent 25 percent of their cash income on food in 1958. For the same kinds and quantities of food that consumers bought in 1941, they would have spent only 16% of their cash income in 1958. It is obvious that our food does cost more. Many factors contribute to this increase besides the additional cost that might be attributed to processing. Consumption of more expensive food items, higher marketing margins, and more food eaten in restaurants are other factors.

The Census of Manufacturers gives some indication of the total bill for processing. The value added by manufacturing of food and kindred products amounted to 3.5 billion of the 20 billion dollars spent for food in 1941. In the year 1958, the comparable figure had climbed to 14 billion dollars.

18. According to the above passage, the cash income of Americans in 1958 was MOST NEARLY _______ billion dollars. 18._____

A. 11.2 B. 17.5 C. 70 D. 280

19. According to the above passage, if Americans bought the same kinds and quantities of food in 1958 as they did in 1941, they would have spent MOST NEARLY _______ billion dollars. 19._____

A. 20 B. 45 C. 74 D. 84

20. According to the above passage, the percent increase in money spent for food in 1958 over 1941, as compared with the percentage increase in money spent for food processing in the same years, 20._____

A. was greater
B. was less
C. was the same
D. cannot be determined from the passage

21. In 1958, an American housewife who bought all of her food ready-to-serve saved in time, as compared with the housewife who prepared all of her food at home 21.

A. 1.6 hours daily
B. 1.9 hours daily
C. 3.5 hours daily
D. an amount of time which cannot be determined from the above passage

Questions 22-25.

DIRECTIONS: Questions 22 through 25 are to be answered SOLELY on the basis of the following passage.

Any member of the retirement system who is in city service, who files a proper application for service credit and agrees to deductions from his compensation at triple his normal rate of contribution, shall be credited with a period of city service previous to the beginning of his present membership in the retirement system. The period of service credited shall be equal to the period throughout which such triple deductions are made, but may not exceed the total of the city service the member rendered between his first day of eligibility for membership in the retirement system and the day he last became a member. After triple contributions for all of the first three years of service credit claimed, the remaining service credit may be purchased by a single payment of the sum of the remaining payments. If the total time purchasable exceeds ten years, triple contributions may be made for one-half of such time, and the remaining time purchased by a single payment of the sum of the remaining payments. Credit for service acquired in the above manner may be used only in determining the amount of any retirement benefit. Eligibility for such benefit will, in all cases, be based upon service rendered after the employee's membership last began, and will be exclusive of service credit purchased as described below.

22. According to the above passage, in order to obtain credit for city service previous to the beginning of an employee's present membership in the retirement system, the employee must 22._

A. apply for the service credit and consent to additional contributions to the retirement system
B. apply for the service credit before he renews his membership in the retirement system
C. have previous city service which does not exceed ten years
D. make contributions to the retirement system for three years

23. According to the information in the above passage, credit for city service previous to the beginning of an employee's present membership in the retirement system, is 23._

A. credited up to a maximum of ten years
B. credited to any member of the retirement system
C. used in determining the amount of the employee's benefits
D. used in establishing the employee's eligibility to receive benefits

24. According to the information in the above passage, a member of the retirement system may purchase service credit for 24.____

A. the period of time between his first day of eligibility for membership in the retirement system and the date he applies for the service credit
B. one-half of the total of his previous city service if the total time exceeds ten years
C. the period of time throughout which triple deductions are made
D. the period of city service between his first day of eligibility for membership in the retirement system and the day he last became a member

25. Suppose that a member of the retirement system has filed an application for service credit for five years of previous city service. 25.____
Based on the information in the above passage, the employee may purchase credit for this previous city service by making

A. triple contributions for three years
B. triple contributions for one-half of the time and a single payment of the sum of the remaining payments
C. triple contributions for three years and a single payment of the sum of the remaining payments
D. a single payment of the sum of the payments

KEY (CORRECT ANSWERS)

1. C
2. D
3. B
4. B
5. A

6. C
7. C
8. D
9. A
10. B

11. D
12. B
13. A
14. B
15. C

16. D
17. C
18. D
19. B
20. B

21. C
22. A
23. C
24. D
25. C

READING COMPREHENSION

UNDERSTANDING AND INTERPRETING WRITTEN MATERIAL

TEST 1

DIRECTIONS FOR THIS SECTION:

All questions are to be answered *SOLELY* on the basis of the information contained in the passage.

Each question or incomplete statement is followed by several suggested answers or completions. Select the one that *BEST* answers the question or completes the statement. *PRINT THE LETTER OF THE CORRECT ANSWER IN THE SPACE AT THE RIGHT.*

Questions 1-7.

Snow-covered roads spell trouble for motorists all winter long. Clearing highways of snow and ice to keep millions of motor vehicles moving freely is a tremendous task. Highway departments now rely, to a great extent, on chemical de-icers to get the big job done. Sodium chloride, in the form of commercial salt, is the de-icer most frequently used.

There is no reliable evidence to prove that salt reduces highway accidents. But available statistics are impressive. For example, before Massachusetts used chemical de-icers, it had a yearly average of 21 fatal accidents and 1,635 injuries attributed to cars skidding on snow or ice. Beginning in 1990, the state began fighting hazardous driving *conditions with* chemical de-icers. During the period 1990-2000, there was a yearly average of only seven deaths and 736 injuries as a result of skids.

Economical and effective in a moderately low temperature range, salt is increasingly popular with highway departments, but not so popular with individual car owners. Salty slush eats away at metal, including auto bodies. It also sprinkles windshields with a fine-grained spray which dries on contact, severely reducing visibility. However, drivers who are hindered or immobilized by heavy winter weather favor the liberal use of products such as sodium chloride. When snow blankets roads, these drivers feel that the quickest way to get back to the safety of driving on bare pavement is through use of de-icing salts.

1. The *MAIN* reason given by the above passage for the use of sodium chloride as a de-icer is that it 1.______
    - A. has no harmful side effects
    - B. is economical
    - C. is popular among car owners
    - D. reduces highway accidents

2. The above passage may *BEST* be described as a(n) 2.______
   A. argument against the use of sodium chloride as a de-icer
   B. discussion of some advantages and disadvantages of sodium chloride as a de-icer
   C. recommendation to use sodium chloride as a de-icer
   D. technical account of the uses and effects of sodium chloride as a de-icer

3. Based on the above passage, the use of salt on snow-covered roadways will eventually 3.______
   A. decrease the efficiency of the automobile fuel
   B. cause tires to deteriorate
   C. damage the surface of the roadway
   D. cause holes in the sides of cars

4. The average number of persons killed yearly in Massachusetts in car accidents caused by skidding on snow or ice, before chemical de-icers were used there, was 4.______
   A. 9 B. 12 C. 21 D. 30

5. According to the passage, it would be advisable to use salt as a de-icer when 5.______
   A. outdoor temperatures are somewhat below freezing
   B. residues on highway surfaces are deemed to be undesirable
   C. snow and ice have low absorbency characteristics
   D. the use of a substance is desired which dries on contact

6. As a result of using chemical de-icers, the number of injuries resulting from skids in Massachusetts was reduced by about 6.______
   A. 35% B. 45% C. 55% D. 65%

7. According to the above passage, driver visibility can be severely reduced by 7.______
   A. sodium chloride deposits on the windshield
   B. glare from salt and snow crystals
   C. salt spray covering the front lights
   D. faulty windshield wipers

Questions 8-10.

An employee should call the Fire Department for any fire except a small one in a wastebasket. This kind of fire can be put out with a fire extinguisher. If the employee is not sure about the size of the fire, he should not wait to find out how big it is. He should call the Fire Department at once.

Every employee should know what to do when a fire starts. He should know how to use the fire-fighting tools in the building and how to call the Fire Department. He should also know where the nearest fire alarm box is. But the most important thing for an employee to do in case of fire is to avoid panic.

8. If there is a small fire in a wastebasket, an employee should 8.______
   A. call the Fire Department
   B. let it burn itself out
   C. open a window
   D. put it out with a fire extinguisher

9. In case of fire, the most important thing for an employee to do is to 9.______
   A. find out how big it is
   B. keep calm
   C. leave the building right away
   D. report to his boss

10. If a large fire starts while he is at work, an employee should *always FIRST* 10.______
    A. call the Fire Department
    B. notify the Housing Superintendent
    C. remove inflammables from the building
    D. use a fire extinguisher

Questions 11-12.

Those correction theorists who are in agreement with severe and rigid controls as a normal part of the correctional process are confronted with a contradiction; this is so because a responsibility which is consistent with freedom cannot be developed in a repressive atmosphere. They do not recognize this contradiction when they carry out their programs with dictatorial force and expect convicted criminals exposed to such programs to be reformed into free and responsible citizens.

11. According to the above paragraph, those correction theorists are faced with a contradiction who 11.______
    A. are in favor of the enforcement of strict controls in a prison
    B. believe that to develop a sense of responsibility, freedom must not be restricted
    C. take the position that the development of responsibility consistent with freedom is not possible in a repressive atmosphere
    D. think that freedom and responsibility can be developed only in a democratic atmosphere

12. According to the above paragraph, a repressive atmosphere in a prison 12.______
    A. does not conform to present-day ideas of freedom of the individual
    B. is admitted by correction theorists to be in conflict with the basic principles of the normal correctional process
    C. is advocated as the best method of maintaining discipline when rehabilitation is of secondary importance
    D. is not suitable for the development of a sense of responsibility consistent with freedom

Questions 13-16.

Abandoned cars – with tires gone, chrome stripped away, and windows smashed – have become a common sight on the City's streets. In 1990, more than 72,000 were deposited at curbs by owners who never came back, an increase of 15,000 from the year before and more than 30 times the number abandoned a decade ago. In January, 1991, the City's Environmental Protection Administrator asked the State Legislature to pass a law requiring a buyer of a new automobile to deposit $100 and an owner of an automobile at the time the law takes effect to deposit $50 with the State Department of Motor Vehicles. In return, they would be given a certificate of deposit which would be passed on to each succeeding owner. The final owner would get the deposit money back if he could present proof that he has disposed of his car "in an environmentally acceptable manner." The Legislature has given no indication that it plans to rush ahead on the matter.

13. The number of cars abandoned in City streets in 1980 was, most nearly, 13.______
    A. 2,500 B. 12,000 C. 27,500 D. 57,000

14. The proposed law would require a person who owned a car bought before the law was passed to deposit 14.______
    A. $100 with the State Department of Motor Vehicles
    B. $50 with the Environmental Protection Administration
    C. $100 with the State Legislature
    D. $50 with the State Department of Motor Vehicles

15. The proposed law would require the State to return the deposit money *only when* the 15.______
    A. original owner of the car shows proof that he sold it
    B. last owner of the car shows proof that he got rid of the car in a satisfactory way
    C. owner of the car shows proof that he has transferred the certificate of deposit to the next owner
    D. last owner of a car returns the certificate of deposit

16. The *main* idea or theme of the above article is that 16.______
    A. a proposed new law would make it necessary for car owners in the State to pay additional taxes
    B. the State Legislature is against a proposed law to require deposits from automobile owners to prevent them from abandoning their cars
    C. the City is trying to find a solution for the increasing number of cars abandoned on its streets
    D. to pay for the removal of abandoned cars, the City's Environmental Protection Administrator has asked the State to fine automobile owners who abandon their vehicles

Questions 17-19.

The German roach is the most common roach in houses in the United States. Adults are pale brown and about 1/2-inch long; both sexes have wings as long as the body, and can be distinguished from other roaches by the two dark stripes on the pronotum. The female carries its egg capsule protruding from her abdomen until the eggs are ready to hatch. This is the only common house-infesting species which carries the egg capsule for such an extended period of time. A female will usually produce 4 to 8 capsules in her lifetime. Each capsule contains 30 to 48 eggs which hatch out in about 28 days at ordinary room temperature. The completion of the nymphal stage under room conditions requires 40 to 125 days. German roaches may live as adults for as long as 303 days.

It is stated about that the German cockroach is the most commonly encountered of the house-infesting species in the United States. The reasons for this are somewhat complex, but the understanding of some of the factors involved are basic to the practice of pest control. In the first place, the German cockroach has a larger number of eggs per capsule and a shorter hatching time than do the other species. It also requires a shorter period from hatching until sexual maturity, so that within a given period of time a population of German roaches will produce a larger number of eggs. On the basis of this fact, we can state that this species has a high reproductive potential. Since the female carries the egg capsule during nearly the entire time that the embryos are developing within the egg, many hazards of the environment which may affect the eggs are avoided. This means that more nymphs are likely to hatch and that a larger portion of the reproductive potential is realized. The nymphs which hatch from each egg capsule tend to stay close to each other, and since they are often close to the female at time of hatching, there is a tendency for the population density to be high locally. Being smaller than most of the other roaches, they are able to conceal themselves in many places which are inaccessible to individuals of the larger species. All of these factors combined help to give the German cockroach an advantage with regard to group survival.

17. According to the above passage, the *most important* feature of the German roach which gives it an advantage over other roaches is its 17._______
    A. distinctive markings
    B. immunity to disease
    C. long life span
    D. power to reproduce

18. An *important* difference between an adult female German roach and an adult female of other species is the 18._______
    A. black bars or stripes which appear on the abdomen of the German roach
    B. German roach's preference for warm, moist places in which to breed
    C. long period of time during which the German roach carries the egg capsule
    D. presence of longer wings on the female German roach

19. A storeroom in a certain housing project has an infestation of German roaches, which includes 125 adult female. If the infestation is not treated and ordinary room temperature is maintained in the storeroom, *how many* eggs will hatch out during the lifetime of these females if they each lay 8 capsules containing 48 eggs each? 19._______
    A. 1,500
    B. 48,000
    C. 96,000
    D. 303,000

Questions 20-22.

City governments have long had building codes which set minimum standards for building and for human occupancy. The code (or series of codes) makes provisions for standards of lighting and ventilation, sanitation, fire prevention, and protection. As a result of demands from manufacturers, builders, real estate people, tenement owners, and building-trades unions, these codes often have established minimum standards well below those that the contemporary society would accept as a rock-bottom minimum. Codes often become outdated, so that meager standards in one era become seriously inadequate a few decades later as society's concept of a minimum standard of living changes. Out-of-date codes, when still in use, have sometimes prevented the introduction of new devices and modern building techniques. Thus, it is extremely important that building codes keep pace with changes in the accepted concept of a minimum standard of living.

20. According to the above passage, all of the following considerations in building planning would probably be covered in a building code *EXCEPT* 20.______
    A. closet space as a percentage of total floor area
    B. size and number of windows required for rooms of differing sizes
    C. placement of fire escapes in each line of apartments
    D. type of garbage disposal units to be installed

21. According to the above passage, if an ideal building code were to be created, how would the established minimum standards in it compare to the ones that are presently set by city governments? They would 21.______
    A. *be lower* than they are at present
    B. *be higher* than they are at present
    C. *be comparable* to the present minimum standards
    D. *vary* according to the economic group that sets them

22. On the basis of the above passage, *what* is the reason for difficulties in introducing new building techniques? 22.______
    A. Builders prefer techniques which represent the rock-bottom minimum desired by society.
    B. Certain manufacturers have obtained patents on various building methods to the exclusion of new techniques.
    C. The government does not want to invest money in techniques that will soon be outdated.
    D. New techniques are not provided for in building codes which are not up to date.

Questions 23-25.

A flameproof fabric is defined as one which, when exposed to small sources of ignition such as sparks or smoldering cigarettes, does not burn beyond the vicinity of the source of the ignition. Cotton fabrics are the materials commonly used that are considered most hazardous. Other materials, such as acetate rayons and linens, are somewhat less hazardous, and woolens and some natural silk fabrics, even when untreated, are about the equal of the average treated cotton fabric insofar as flame spread and ease of ignition are concerned. The method of application is to immerse the fabric in a flameproofing solution. The container used must be large enough so that all the fabric is thoroughly wet and there are no folds which the solution does not penetrate.

23. According to the above paragraph, a flameproof fabric is one which 23.______
   A. is unaffected by heat and smoke
   B. resists the spread of flames when ignited
   C. burns with a cold flame
   D. cannot be ignited by sparks or cigarettes
   E. may smolder but cannot burn

24. According to the above paragraph, woolen fabrics which have not been flameproofed are as likely to catch fire as 24.______
   A. treated silk fabrics
   B. treated acetate rayon fabrics
   C. untreated linen fabrics
   D. untreated synthetic fabrics
   E. treated cotton fabrics

25. In the method described above, the flameproofing solution is *BEST* applied to the fabric by 25.______
   A. sponging the fabric
   B. spraying the fabric
   C. dipping the fabric
   D. brushing the fabric
   E. sprinkling the fabric

KEY (CORRECT ANSWERS)

1. B
2. B
3. D
4. C
5. A
6. C
7. A
8. D
9. B
10. A
11. A
12. D
13. A
14. D
15. B
16. C
17. D
18. C
19. B
20. A
21. B
22. D
23. B
24. E
25. C

TEST 2

DIRECTIONS FOR THIS SECTION:

All questions are to be answered *SOLELY* on the basis of the information contained in the passage.

Each question or incomplete statement is followed by several suggested answers or completions. Select the one that *BEST* answers the question or completes the statement. *PRINT THE LETTER OF THE CORRECT ANSWER IN THE SPACE AT THE RIGHT.*

Questions 1-4.

Safety belts provide protection for the passengers of a vehicle by preventing them from crashing around inside if the vehicle is involved in a collision. They operate on the principle similar to that used in the packaging of fragile items. You become a part of the vehicle package and you are kept from being tossed about inside if the vehicle is suddenly decelerated. Many injury-causing collisions at low speeds – for example, at city intersections – could have been injury-free if the occupants had fastened their safety belts. There is a double advantage to the driver in that it not only protects him from harm, but prevents him from being yanked away from the wheel, thereby permitting him to maintain control of the car. Since, without seat belts, the risk of injury is about 50% greater, and the risk of death is about 30% greater, the State Vehicle and Traffic Law provided that a motor vehicle manufactured or assembled after June 30, 1964 and designated as a 1965 or later model should have two safety belts for the front seat. It also provides that a motor vehicle manufactured after June 30, 1966 and designated as a 1967 or later model should have at least one safety belt for the rear seat for each passenger for which the rear seat of such vehicle was designed.

1. The principle on which seat belts work is that 1.______
   A. a car and its driver and passengers are fragile
   B. a person fastened to the car will not be thrown around when the car slows down suddenly
   C. the driver and passengers of a car that is suddenly decelerated will be thrown forward
   D. the driver and passengers of an automobile should be packaged the way fragile items are packaged

2. We can assume from the above passage that safety belts should be worn at all times because you can never tell when 2.______
   A. a car will be forced to turn off onto another road
   B. it will be necessary to shift into low gear to go up a hill
   C. you will have to speed up to pass another car
   D. a car may have to come to a sudden stop

3. Besides preventing injury, an *additional* benefit from the use of safety belts is that 3.______
   A. collisions are fewer
   B. damage to the car is kept down
   C. the car can be kept under control
   D. the number of accidents at city intersections is reduced

4. The risk of death in car accidents for people who don't use safety belts is 4.______
   A. 30% greater than the risk of injury
   B. 30% greater than for those who do use them
   C. 50% less than the risk of injury
   D. 50% greater than for those who use them

Questions 5-9.

Any person who is living in New York City and is otherwise eligible may be granted public assistance whether or not he has New York State residence. However, since New York City does not contribute to the cost of assistance granted to persons who are without State residence, the cases of all recipients must be formally identified as to whether or not each member of the household has State residence.

To acquire State residence a person must have resided in New York State continuously for one year. Such residence is not lost unless the person is out of the State continuously for a period of one year or longer. Continuous residence does not include any period during which the individual is a patient in a hospital, an inmate of a public institution or of an incorporated private institution, a resident on a military reservation, or a minor residing in a boarding home while under the care of an authorized agency. Receipt of public assistance does not prevent a person from acquiring State residence. State residence, once acquired, is not lost because of absence from the State while a person is serving in the U. S. Armed Forces or the Merchant Marine; nor does a member of the family of such a person lose State residence while living with or near that person in these circumstances.

Each person, regardless of age, acquires or loses State residence as an individual. There is no derivative State residence except for an infant at the time of birth. He is deemed to have State residence if he is in the custody of both parents and either one of them has State residence, or if the parent having custody of him has State residence.

5. According to the above passage, an infant is deemed to have New York State residence at the time of his birth if 5.______
   A. he is born in New York State but neither of his parents is a resident
   B. he is in the custody of only one parent, who is not a resident, but his other parent is a resident
   C. his brother and sister are residents
   D. he is in the custody of both his parents but only one of them is a resident

6. The Jones family consists of five members. Jack and Mary Jones have lived in New York State continuously for the past eighteen months after having lived in Ohio since they were born. Of their three children, one was born ten months ago and has been in the custody of his parents since birth. Their second child lived in Ohio until six months ago and then moved in with his parents. Their third child had never lived in New York until he moved with his parents to New York eighteen months ago. However, he entered the armed forces one month later and has not lived in New York since that time. 6.______
   Based on the above passage, how many members of the Jones family are New York State residents?
   A. 2 B. 3 C. 4 D. 5

7. Assuming that each of the following individuals has lived continuously in New York State for the past year, and has never previously lived in the State, *which one* of them is a New York State resident? 7.______
   A. Jack Salinas, who has been an inmate in a State correctional facility for six months of the year
   B. Fran Johnson, who has lived on an Army base for the entire year
   C. Arlene Snyder, who married a non-resident during the past year
   D. Gary Phillips, who was a patient in a Veterans Administration hospital for the entire year

8. The above passage implies that the reason for determining whether or not a recipient of public assistance is a State resident is that 8.______
   A. the cost of assistance for non-residents is not a New York City responsibility
   B. non-residents living in New York City are not eligible for public assistance
   C. recipients of public assistance are barred from acquiring State residence
   D. New York City is responsible for the full cost of assistance to recipients who are residents

9. Assume that the Rollins household in New York City consists of six members at the present time – Anne Rollins, her three children, her aunt, and her uncle. Anne Rollins and one of her children moved to New York City seven months ago. Neither of them had previously lived in New York State. Her other two children have lived in New York City continuously for the past two years, as has her aunt. Anne Rollins' uncle had lived in New York City continuously for many years until two years ago. He then entered the armed forces and has returned to New York City within the past month. Based on the above passage, how many members of the Rollins' household are New York State residents? 9.______
   A. 2 B. 3 C. 4 D. 6

Questions 10-12.

The agreement under which a tenant rents property from a landlord is known as a lease. Generally speaking, leases are classified as either short-term or long-term in duration. They are further subdivided according to the method used to determine the amount of periodic rent payments. Of the many types of lease in use, the more commonly used ones are the following:

1. The straight or fixed lease is one in which rent may be paid in equal amounts throughout the duration of the lease. These are usually restricted to short-term leasing, or somewhat longer-term if clauses in the lease provide for periodic escalation of payments as the economy shifts.
2. Percentage leasing, used for short-term commercial leasing, provides the landlord with a stipulated percentage of a tenant's gross sales from goods and services sold on the premises, in addition to a fixed amount of rent.
3. The net lease, generally long-term (ten years or more), requires the tenant to pay all operating costs, including real estate taxes and insurance. In a net-net lease, the tenant further agrees to meet mortgage interest and principal payments.

4. An escalated lease, which is a long-term lease, requires rent to be of a stipulated base amount which periodically is subject to escalation in accordance with cost-of-living index scales, or in direct proportion to taxes, insurance, and operating costs.

10. Based on the information given in the passage, *which* type of lease is *most likely* to be advantageous to a landlord if there is a high rate of inflation? 10.______
    A. fixed lease
    B. percentage lease
    C. net lease
    D. escalated lease

11. On the basis of the above passage, *which* types of lease would generally be *MOST* suitable for a well-established textile company which requires permanent facilities for its large operations? 11.______
    A. Percentage lease and escalated lease
    B. Escalated lease and net lease
    C. Straight lease and net lease
    D. Straight lease and percentage lease

12. According to the above passage, the *only* type of lease which assures the same amount of rent throughout a specified interval is the 12.______
    A. straight lease
    B. percentage lease
    C. net-net lease
    D. escalated lease

Questions 13-18.

Basic to every office is the need for proper lighting. Inadequate lighting is a familiar cause of fatigue and serves to create a somewhat dismal atmosphere in the office. One requirement of proper lighting is that it be of an appropriate intensity. Intensity is measured in foot-candles. According to the Illuminating Engineering Society of New York, for casual seeing tasks such as in reception rooms, inactive file rooms, and other service areas, it is recommended that the amount of light be 30 foot-candles. For ordinary seeing tasks such as reading and work in active file rooms and in mail rooms, the recommended lighting is 100 foot-candles. For very difficult seeing tasks such as accounting, transcribing, and business-machine use, the recommended lighting is 150 foot-candles.

Lighting intensity is only one requirement. Shadows and glare are to be avoided. For example, the larger the proportion of a ceiling filled with lighting units, the more glare-free and comfortable the lighting will be. Natural lighting from windows is not too dependable because on dark wintry days windows yield little usable light, and on sunny, summer afternoons the glare from windows may be very distracting. Desks should not face the windows. Finally, the main lighting source ought to be overhead and to the left of the user.

13. According to the above passage, insufficient light in the office may cause 13.______
    A. glare
    B. shadows
    C. tiredness
    D. distraction

14. Based on the above passage, *which* of the following must be considered when planning lighting arrangements? The 14.______
    A. amount of natural light present
    B. amount of work to be done
    C. level of difficulty of work to be done
    D. type of activity to be carried out

15. It can be inferred from the above passage that a well-coordinated lighting scheme is likely to result in 15.______
    A. greater employee productivity
    B. elimination of light reflection
    C. lower lighting cost
    D. more use of natural light

16. Of the following, the *BEST* title for the above passage is: 16.______
    A. Characteristics of Light
    B. Light Measurement Devices
    C. Factors to Consider When Planning Lighting Systems
    D. Comfort vs. Cost When Devising Lighting Arrangements

17. According to the above passage, a foot-candle is a measurement of the 17.______
    A. number of bulbs used
    B. strength of the light
    C. contrast between glare and shadow
    D. proportion of the ceiling filled with lighting units

18. According to the above passage, the number of foot-candles of light that would be needed to copy figures onto a payroll is 18.______
    A. less than 30 foot-candles
    B. 30 foot-candles
    C. 100 foot-candles
    D. 150 foot-candles

Questions 19-22.

A summons is an official statement ordering a person to appear in court. In traffic violation situations, summonses are used when arrests need not be made. The main reason for traffic summonses is to deter motorists from repeating the same traffic violation. Occasionally, motorists may make unintentional driving errors and sometimes they are unaware of correct driving regulations. In cases such as these, the policy should be to have the Officer verbally inform the motorist of the violation and warn him against repeating it. The purpose of this practice is not to limit the number of summonses, but rather to prevent the issuing of summonses when the violation is not due to deliberate intent or to inexcusable negligence.

19. According to the above passage, the *PRINCIPAL* reason for issuing traffic summonses is to 19.______
    A. discourage motorists from violating these laws again
    B. increase the money collected by the city
    C. put traffic violators in prison
    D. have them serve as substitutes for police officers

20. The reason a verbal warning may sometimes be substituted for a summons is to 20.______
    A. limit the number of summonses
    B. distinguish between excusable and inexcusable violations
    C. provide harsher penalties for deliberate intent than for inexcusable negligence
    D. decrease the caseload in the courts

21. The author of the above passage feels that someone who violated a traffic regulation because he did *not* know about the regulation should be 21.______
    - A. put under arrest
    - B. fined less money
    - C. given a summons
    - D. told not to do it again

22. Using the distinctions made by the author of the above passage, the *one* of the following motorists to whom it would be *MOST* desirable to issue a summons is the one who exceeded the speed limit because he 22.______
    - A. did not know the speed limit
    - B. was late for an important business appointment
    - C. speeded to avoid being hit by another car
    - D. had a speedometer which was not working properly

Questions 23-25.

Physical design plays a very significant role in crime rate. Crime rate has been found to increase almost proportionately with building height. The average number of crimes is much greater in higher buildings than in lower ones (equal to or less than six stories). What is most interesting is that in buildings of six stories or less, the project size or total number of units does not make a difference. It seems that, although larger projects encourage crime by fostering feelings of anonymity, isolation, irresponsibility, and lack of identity with surroundings, evidence indicates that larger projects encompassed in low buildings seem to offset what we may assume to be factors conducive to high crime rates. High-rise projects not only experience a higher rate of crime within the buildings, but a greater proportion of the crime occurs in the interior public spaces of these buildings as compared with those of the lower buildings. Lower buildings have more limited public space than higher ones. A criminal probably perceives that the interior public areas of buildings are where his victims are most vulnerable and where the possibility of his being seen or apprehended is minimal. Placement of elevators, entrance lobbies, fire stairs and secondary exits all are factors related to the likelihood of crimes taking place in buildings. The study of all of these elements should bear some weight in the planning of new projects.

23. According to the passage, *which* of the following *BEST* describes the relationship between building size and crime? 23.______
    - A. Larger projects lead to a greater crime rate
    - B. Higher buildings tend to increase the crime rate
    - C. The smaller the number of project apartments in low buildings the higher the crime rate
    - D. Anonymity and isolation serve to lower the crime rate in small buildings

24. According to the passage, the likelihood of a criminal attempting a mugging in the interior public portions of a high-rise building is good because 24.______
    - A. tenants will be constantly flowing in and out of the area
    - B. there is easy access to fire stairs and secondary exits
    - C. there is a good chance that no one will see him
    - D. tenants may not recognize the victims of crime as their neighbors

25. *Which* of the following is *implied* by the passage as an explanation for the fact that the crime rate is lower in large low-rise housing projects than in large high-rise projects? 25.______

A. Tenants know each other better and take a greater interest in what happens in the project
B. There is more public space where tenants are likely to gather together
C. The total number of units in a low-rise project is fewer than the total number of units in a high-rise project
D. Elevators in low-rise buildings travel quickly, thus limiting the amount of time in which a criminal can act

---

KEY (CORRECT ANSWERS)

1. B
2. D
3. C
4. B
5. D

6. B
7. C
8. A
9. C
10. D

11. B
12. A
13. C
14. D
15. A

16. C
17. B
18. D
19. A
20. B

21. D
22. B
23. B
24. C
26. A

UNDERSTANDING, INTERPRETING AND PREPARING WRITTEN MATERIAL

TABLE OF CONTENTS

UNDERSTANDING, INTERPRETING AND PREPARING WRITTEN MATERIAL

I. HOW TO DEVELOP YOUR READING ABILITIES

A. COMMENTARY

Reading is the most important learning skill one can acquire for success and enjoyment throughout life. It is an integral part of our personal and working lives. Consider how much time everyday is spent reading newspapers, letters, books, menus, directions, or signs. Eighty-five percent of college work, for example, involves reading. The better you read, the more you will succeed in study or work and enjoy the time you spend with books.

Reading is basically the understanding of words and the association between them. To improve your reading skills, you must increase your ability to see and understand the grouping of words, or ideas, at a speed and in a manner that is comfortable for you. To be a good reader, concentrate on what you are doing and learn to use your eyes to the best of your ability. Move them at a rate that allows your brain to absorb the main ideas printed on a page. Bad readers are usually distracted and read each word without grasping the relationship between them. This causes them to retrace or reread the material.

Most people do not perfect their reading after the fifth grade. High school or college students are often bad readers. They overlook the need to continually use and improve good reading habits. Remember your eyes, like fingers for the piano or legs for skiing, must be trained to be skillful.

If you would like to improve your reading skills, these seven steps can help:

1. Evaluate your reading habits
2. Provide the right atmosphere
3. Use your eyes efficiently
4. Continue to broaden your vocabulary
5. Adapt your speed so you understand the material
6. Practice on a regular basis
7. Enrich your life with good books

B. EVALUATING YOUR READING HABITS

Analyze your present reading habits so that you know where to improve your skills:

Do you use your lips, throat, or mind to "vocalize" words?	You are probably still using the childhood habit of sounding out each word. This slows you down.
Do strange words constantly stop your progress?	Your vocabulary needs improving.
Do you read every single word?	You should train your eyes to span phrases or "thought units" instead of individual words.
Do you go back over what you have read?	You are not paying attention. Good concentration means good comprehension
Do you always read at the same speed?	Speed should vary depending on the material and your purpose for reading, e.g., fiction, newspapers, textbooks.

Has your reading speed and comprehension remained static for a number of years?	Skillful reading is an art and needs continual practice. The more you read, the more you will enjoy and remember.

C. PROVIDING THE PROPER PHYSICAL CLIMATE

Your approach to reading, whether it is for pleasure, information, or study, will influence your ability to do it well. Learn to enjoy rt in an atmosphere conducive to reading.

Choose *an area where you can read with a minimum of interruption.* This should include proper light, a pencil for marking highlights in books or taking notes, and a dictionary near at hand.

Location *and posture can influence your attitude.* Sitting up in a good chair will make you more alert. Reading in bed is usually not the place to concentrate since it is an area associated with relaxation and sleep.

Average readers should hold a book about fifteen inches away from their eyes. It should be held on a slant for optimum viewing.

The sounds of radio, television or music are distracting. You can understand and remember better when your full attention is given to the process of reading.

D. USING YOUR EYES EFFICIENTLY

It is the eyes that see printed words and transmit them to the brain. Understand how they work and give them the opportunity to perform well. Eyes perceive words only when they stop moving or make what is called a "fixation." It is during this pause that the brain records what the eyes have seen. Depending upon your "eye span" you will perceive one, two or more words in each fixation. The average college student, for example, has a span of 1.1 words and makes four fixations per second.

Vocalizing words impedes reading progress. Poor readers are inclined to whisper, use their lips, enunciate silently in their throats, or visualize the words in their minds. If you have any of these bad habits, they should be broken because they slow down understanding. Learn to move your eyes continually forward at a pace that allows your brain to understand the meaning of the printed matter.

Train *your eyes to increase their span by taking in more than one word at a time.* You can make your eyes fix on related words, phrases, or short lines in one brief stop. This sentence, for example, should be read in five fixations: "The cost of oil/has risen/because of/ limited national resources/and increased imports."

Don't allow your eyes to go back over words. Think about what you are seeing and keep on going at a speed that is fast enough to remember at the end what you read at the beginning. Faster reading, with no retracing, helps comprehension. This does not, of course, mean you cannot review what you have just read.

Many people need glasses to read well. Blurred words, continual eye fatigue or itching, and stinging eyes might mean you need glasses. If you think your eyes need correction, have them examined by an eye doctor. If glasses are prescribed, do not hesitate to buy and wear them. Make sure they are always free of dirt and scratches.

E. BROADENING YOUR VOCABULARY

The person with a good grasp of words is usually a good reader and a good student. Words are the basis of human communication and enable people to convey their thoughts and emotions to each other. This is why the first word uttered by a child generates such joy and pride in the parent. It is proof positive that this little being has the ability to communicate as a human.

1. *Vocabulary should grow as you mature.* At every grade level and stage of life, it is necessary to increase the number and understanding of words. Get to know their structure, that they are composed of roots, prefixes and suffixes, each with its own meaning.

2. *Knowing the origin of words helps in understanding new ones.* Most English words derive from Latin or Greek. This is why some knowledge of these languages is helpful. If you know the derivation of a word's parts, then you will be able to analyze its meaning, e.g., biography, a written account of a person's life, comes from two Greek words: bios meaning life and graphein meaning write.

3. *Always have a dictionary nearby* whether you are reading for pleasure or for work. When you are reading textbooks or technical books, familiarize yourself with the glossary that is sometimes printed in the back to define special words. Use it whenever necessary.

4. *Maintain a list of new words you see or hear.* Be on the lookout for ones you don't know. Jot them down, look them up, and then make a point of using them in writing or speaking at least twice as soon as you can. At the end of a month, review your list and see whether you remember their meanings and how to use them. It can be a private game that is fun and rewarding.

F. ADAPTING YOUR SPEED FOR UNDERSTANDING

A good reader must learn to balance speed with accuracy. Don't expect to read everything at the same rate. Like a well-tuned car, your eyes must adapt to the terrain. Above all, you must understand and remember what you are reading.

1. *Read with a purpose, be aware of what you are reading and why.* Your speed should be adjusted to the type of material. Don't expect to whiz through a chapter of biology at the same rate as a chapter of a novel.

2. *Scanning material first can be helpful in nearly all types of* reading. Get in the habit of surveying headlines, chapter headings, and subheads first. Look for the main ideas. Next you will want to know the important details that support them. Read carefully the first and last paragraphs, which should state the most important facts and conclusions. You should read the straight material in between at a faster rate that allows you to understand the matter in as much depth as you want. Just remember to keep your eyes moving forward.

If *you are reading for enjoyment, you can skim more easily over* the lines, paragraphs, and pages. It is not important that you take in every word or sentence in depth. As in most writing, each paragraph usually has one main idea supported by details in which you may or may not be interested. Try to span as many words as possible with a continuous rhythm of eye movements or fixations.

3. *When you read a newspaper or magazine, or non-fiction, you want to grasp the highlights and some details.* This kind of reading is for general information. It differs from your leisure reading because the material is more serious, not so light or as easy to comprehend as fiction. But it still might not be necessary to take in every word or every sentence completely.

4. *When reading a text, first survey the entire book.* Look over the table of contents, chapter headlines, and subheads. Get an overview of the author's objectives by reading the introduction and preface.

5. *Studying requires close reading* because you will need to remember more details to support the main ideas. Read each chapter for the important concepts and as many details as necessary to comprehend the material. Underline major points and make margin notes to highlight your observations. After you have finished reading, question yourself, review the summary if there is one, and then look back to see whether you have understood the material.

6. *Graphic material can help reading comprehension.* Do not overlook the importance of tables, maps, graphs, drawings, and photographs which are included to reinforce your understanding of the text.

G. PRACTICING ON A REGULAR BASIS

Like any skill, reading requires practice. In order to develop the habit of good reading, you must train your eyes and mind to perform well together. You don't have to take a speed reading course. The rewards will be most worthwhile if you take the time and persevere.

1. *Set aside 15 to 30 minutes every day to practice reading*, much as a pianist, typist, or golfer would. Start off your exercises with light material, such as READER'S DIGEST, that has uniform page length and short articles. Your objective is to read with understanding at your best speed.

2. *There are established norms against which you may test yourself.* The speeds generally accepted for average readers are: easy or light material, 250-350 words per minute (wpm); medium to difficult material, 200-250 wpm; and difficult material, 100-150 wpm.

3. *Time yourself exactly for two pages* with a clock that has a second hand. Calculate the minutes and seconds and divide the time into the number of words on the page. This will tell you what your current reading speed is in words per minute. You can get the average number of words on a page by taking the average per line and multiplying it by the number of lines, omitting headings. Using the opposite page as an example: the average number of words per line is 11, with 40 lines of type, totalling 440 words on the page. If you read it in 1 minute and 45 seconds (105 seconds), you read 4 words a second, or 240 words per minute.

4. *Ask yourself questions on the material and review it* to see whether you are correct. If you miss important details, your speed is probably too fast for your present reading ability. Don't get discouraged, just keep practicing.

5. *Read 3 or 4 articles each day for two or three weeks.* Use the same length and type of material each day. Push yourself but use discretion, making sure you check your comprehension of the material. Record your speed faithfully each time so you can check your progress.

6. *Then switch to something more difficult in vocabulary, style, and content.* Do this for two more weeks, questioning yourself and recording your time. After a total of six weeks, you should have increased your reading ability considerably.

7. *Try to get your speed on easy material to about 300 words per minute.* Once you have reached this level, you will know you can do as well as the average good reader.

8. *Maintain the habit by reading at least a half hour a day.* You will be enriched by keeping up with newspapers, magazines, and books. You will also enjoy reading more as your proficiency increases.

II. HOW TO USE YOUR BOOKS

A. COMMENTARY

A textbook, properly used, can be invaluable to you in any course. It can make the course easier. It can add to the knowledge you gain in class as well as prepare you for successful classroom work. It can and should serve as a permanent resource book after the course itself has been completed. The following six steps have proved to be very helpful in using textbooks, and they can be applied to any book or assignment:

1. Survey the entire book
2. Read for the main ideas
3. Question yourself as you read
4. Underline and take notes
5. Use study guides
6. Review systematically

B. SURVEYING THE ENTIRE BOOK

Don't start right in reading your textbook from page one. First, make a quick survey of the entire book to get an idea of what your text is all about.

1. *Look through the entire book.* See how it is put together. Note the chapter headings and subheadings, any reference reading suggestions, quizzes, dates, discussion questions, graphs, pictures, diagrams, summaries, or other aids which the author has put in to help you understand and remember the text.

2. *Read the preface.* Here the author usually will tell you the main purpose in writing the book, his/her outlook and approach to the material.

3. Scan *the table of contents.* This will show you how the book is organized and how much material is covered. Keep looking back at the table of contents after you have read certain chapters to remind yourself of the author's entire plan.

4. *Look over the last chapter or final few pages* of the book. The author will often summarize the main points made in the separate chapters.

5. *Survey each chapter.* Before you read an assigned chapter, make a rapid preview of the material. Look for any headnotes or summaries that may be included. They give valuable clues to the main ideas the author wants to emphasize, and also serve as a handy outline. Take special note of chapter headings and subheadings. The way they are arranged will often tell you which are the main topics and which are the less important ones.

C. READING FOR THE MAIN IDEAS

Your reading should have a primary purpose–to find out what the author's main ideas are in any chapter. Keep asking, as if you are talking to the author, just what is he trying to get across. Don't worry about the details. By concentrating on the main ideas, you will find the details much easier to remember.

1. *Read your assignment before the class discussion.* If you read the assignment beforehand and then join in the classroom discussion, you will clarify ideas and gain confidence in your own ability. If you wait until the professor and other students discuss a topic before you read it, you will lose faith in yourself as an independent reader. When you put your ideas into words, the material you have read will become more meaningful and will be remembered much longer. Cramming for examinations will be unnecessary.

2. *Coordinate class notes with reading.* Tie-in your reading with your class or lecture notes. If you keep full, clear, and accurate notes, you will find the ideas and concepts you got from your textbook reading will become much clearer. Moreover, a well-kept lecture notebook can become as important a part of your permanent collection for future reference as your textbook.

3 *Summarize whatever you have read. After* finishing a page, restate the main ideas in your mind and then glance back to see whether you are correct. Before closing the text, repeat the major points of the material just read. See whether you can jot down the central ideas in the section completed. If you can, most of the supporting details will return to you rather easily. When you resume your reading the next day, your brief review will serve as an encouragement to begin the next assignment. By noting the major points of your reading, you will find preparation for an exam a relatively simple matter.

D. QUESTIONING YOURSELF AS YOU READ

When you read the text material, imagine you are having a discussion with the author. Keep asking him questions about the statements being made and ideas presented. See whether he is giving answers that satisfy you.

1. *What* is the meaning of the title of the chapter, what are the meanings of the headings and subheadings, what do the important words mean in their context, what do the tables, diagrams, or graphs try to demonstrate, what do the concluding remarks mean?

If it is literature you are reading, what is the meaning of the title, from what point of view is the author writing, what is the setting, the historical period, the tone, mood, and style? Is symbolism being used to convey a message?

2. *Why* did the author choose to develop ideas in this particular order; why did he spend so much time on certain points?

3. *How* would you rate the effectiveness of the author's style of presentation? Does he use humor, exaggeration, irony, satire? Are many examples used? Are the graphs and pictures appropriate and easy to understand?

4. *For whom* is the author writing? If he is writing a history text, is he trying to influence the reader's point of view? If he is dealing with psychology, does he belong to a special school of thought and does this attitude shape his ideas?

5. *When* was the book written? Have new developments rendered the author's opinion out of date?

6. *Ask questions in class.* Bring specific inquiries raised by your reading to class and pose them to the professor and to other students. Make certain you are an active participant and that your reading plays an active part in your classroom work.

E. UNDERLINING AND TAKING NOTES

1. *Mark your text freely* and underline key statements. Bracket key phrases and put light check marks around significant points. After you have read a few paragraphs, return to your markings and underline the phrases and sentences that seem most important. Be careful to select only the main ideas. If you underline well, you will have a clear picture of the most important material when you review.

2. *Writing in the margins can also be helpful.* Challenge the author directly in the margins of the text. Ask questions, disagree, change statements, rephrase concepts in your own language. By actively engaging the author's ideas, you will read more alertly and remember what you have read.

3. *Note taking is an individual matter* and each student will have to decide what the best technique is for himself. There is no question that to make learning active and to retain what you have read, you must take notes. These notes will be very useful at a later time, reminding you of your immediate reaction to specific passages in the textbook and reviving rnformation you have forgotten.

4. *A journal or reading log can be useful.* After you have read a section or a chapter, record your thoughts so you will have a personal and active encounter with the textbook. You may want to keep an informal reading log, jotting down perceptions or expressing yourself creatively. You may want to be more formal and synopsize whole chapters in a brief paragraph. In any event, the transfer of your thoughts to paper will be of great help in reviewing and in writing essays or term papers later on.

F. USING STUDY GUIDES

Study guides, outlines, and supplements which accompany many texts are extremely helpful. *These guides often give synopses of the material* and raise provocative questions that make you see far more deeply into the textbook itself. Use the best study guides and supplements available and refer to them as you read. Return to them when you review for an exam.

Text supplements that are mentioned in the author's suggested *additional readings or bibliography should be consulted.* Often a point that seems obscure in your text can be clarified by a special study of the subject.

G. REVIEWING SYSTEMATICALLY

Reviewing is a cumulative discipline and ought to become a habit of study. You *review* a phrase or sentence by underlining it. You review a page after reading it by simply recalling the major points. You reassess the meaning of a chapter by noting some of the main ideas on a piece of paper. You *re-evaluate* the material when in class by joining in the discussion. You *record* varied points of view and interpretations in your notebook as you listen to the professor and other students. You make your final review before the test by re-examining your own textbook underlinings, your notes in the margins, lecture materials, and notebooks.

1. *Avoid cramming* at all costs, even though it may be tempting to postpone assignments and wait until the night before the examination. Cramming creates tension that may hinder your memory during the examination and will certainly prevent you from remembering afterwards.

2. The easiest way of reviewing is to *assemble your summary notes* of each chapter, converting the statements into questions, and checking the individual chapters to see whether you are answering the questions fully and accurately. Your questions in the margins and underlinings will help you to recall details. If you have kept a reading journal, your own reflections will be a further aid in remembering particular ideas. Your class notes will reinforce your reading. Pose rigorous questions to yourself, but, as you approach the examination, remember one important point–*do not clutter your mind with details.* If you have read the text carefully and can identify major ideas, you will easily remember supporting information and data.

III. HOW TO DEVELOP YOUR WRITING ABILITIES

A. COMMENTARY

A renowned author has said that writing is an act of faith. Undoubtedly, he meant that, to express yourself well, you must have faith in yourself, and in your thoughts and in your ability to express them. The key is to be confident and competent enough to convey those thoughts to the reader.

Admittedly, that is easier said than done. Writing, like any skill worth mastering, takes practice and work. But the process of improving your writing can be fun and challenging, and the benefits well worth the effort. After all, in tests or exams you should be able to write clearly about what you have learned. Or, when your friends are away, you should be able to write them interesting letters. And later, when you are working, the ability to express yourself will be invaluable–in a letter to a prospective employer, for example, or in office correspondence, business reports, or sales proposals.

This section is an overview of the techniques of writing. It reviews the main elements of grammar and the principles of good composition–the framework upon which you build your skills:

1. Choose words carefully
2. Punctuate, capitalize, and spell correctly
3. Construct sentences and paragraphs clearly
4. Appraise and outline each assignment
5. Write, review, and revise

B. CHOOSING WORDS CAREFULLY

To understand others and be understood by all, know the big words but use the small.

Anonymous

Have you ever thought of yourself as a word worker? Actually, we all are. It is through words that we express our thoughts or emotions, Without words, we would be unable to record, preserve, explain, or en-joy the learning of the ages. Man's unique ability to communicate effectively depends upon a familiarity and facility with words.

Imagine carpenters, whose livelihood depends upon the ability to work with wood. Before they can build anything, they must learn how to handle the raw material of their trade. First, they study the different kinds of wood: their uses, their textures, and their weaknesses and strengths. Through practice, they learn to cut, shape, and smooth their work so that it serves the purpose for which it is intended.

So it is with words, the raw material of language. First, we must recognize the eight types, or parts of speech: nouns,* pronouns, adjectives, verbs, adverbs, prepositions, conjunctions, and interjections. The more familiar we become with each of these–and with their particular function and their qualities–the easier it is to use them correctly.

* Words underscored are defined in the Glossary.

Through practice, you will learn how to use words accurately and effectively. You will know, for instance, to rely on concrete nouns and on strong, active verbs for impact. You will use passive verbs less frequently since they can lack strength and character. You will come to understand that if you are precise in your choice of nouns and verbs, you will have no need to add qualifying adverbs or adjectives to make yourself understood.

A competent writer is one who uses qualifying words or phrases sparingly. Sentences built with strength and precision require no patching or additional support. More forceful writing uses the positive rather than negative. It is also better to avoid colloquial, foreign, or slang expressions because they can interrupt the smooth flow of English.

One of the best ways to improve your facility with words is to keep a dictionary nearby. You will find in it not only definitions and spelling, but derivations, synonyms, pronunciation, and word usage. If you acquire the habit of looking up new words, you will expand your vocabulary and will better understand the subtleties of meaning. Accuracy in the use of words is a very important aspect of a writer's skill.

If you look again at some of the good books you have read, you will probably notice that the words used are exact in their meaning, and that the language carries you forward without interruption. Long descriptions can be boring. Clear and concise writing makes for more interesting reading. When you write, keep your readers in mind.

C. PUNCTUATING, CAPITALIZING AND SPELLING CORRECTLY

It's not wise to violate rules until you know how to observe them.

T. S. Eliot

We use punctuation, capitalization, and correct spelling to make our writing as readable and clear to others as possible. These visual aids are integral parts of our written language, and it is important to know the basic rules that govern them.

Punctuation clarifies meaning and gives expression to writing. Properly used-not overused-punctuation marks help readers understand what is before them by separating or setting off related words, phrases, or clauses. The nine main punctuation marks might be compared to the glue or nails carpenters use to join their work. A writer uses marks to cement or to separate related words and phrases. They identify the point at which one complete thought, or part of one, begins or ends.

Capitalization is another visual aid to a reader's understanding. Capital letters denote, for instance, a proper name or title, or the beginning of a sentence, a line of poetry, or a quotation. They help to reinforce the purpose of punctuation marks such as periods or semicolons. Some accomplished poets and authors take the liberty of ignoring the rules, but most of us should not. The omission of punctuation marks or capitals, in non-fiction writing especially, is incorrect and an indication of bad composition. If you have a doubt, you can find the answer quickly by referring to a basic grammar or a book of rhetoric.

Spelling, of course, is also vital to correct word usage. Most English words are derived from Latin or Greek words, or roots. A spelling error, therefore, might indicate carelessness or inaccurate knowledge of a word. If you do not understand the meaning of the prefixes un and in, for example, you might distort the use of a word in a sentence. The thought, The person who beats a dog is inhuman, would be incorrect if the word unhuman were used. Uncertainty about a word can usually be quickly resolved by referring to a dictionary.

D. CONSTRUCTING CLEAR SENTENCES AND SMOOTH PARAGRAPHS

Word carpentry is like any other kind of carpentry: you must join your sentences smoothly.

Anatole France

A sentence is a unit of thought expressed by a word, or related words. The clearer sentences are and the smoother their sequence, the more interesting they will be. You want to make sure that your reader knows what you are writing about (the subject) and what you have to say about it (the predicate). Each sentence must have a main idea. Through the use of phrases and clauses, you introduce other subordinate ideas.

Depending upon the amount of detail and explanation it presents, a sentence can vary in construction. It will be what grammarians refer to as a simple, compound, or complex form of sentence. But, whatever the style, related words should be kept together. Misplaced modifiers are often the culprits in obscure writing because it is not clear which word or phrase they modify. For example: *The girl went walking in the blue hat.* The phrase *in the blue* hat should be placed after the word girl, which it modifies.

You should always keep your readers in mind and make it possible for them to understand you easily. Keep the verb close to the subject. Try to avoid unnecessary words that might detract from the main verb or action of the sentence. Also, take special care with pronouns. Place them in the sentence so that it is clear to which noun or pronoun they refer. For example: *Mary and Polly were reading her poem.* Whoset poem is being read? To clear up the confusion you might write *Mary was reading her poem with Polly.*

Writing is more interesting if the length and style of sentences vary. After a number of long statements, make a point of using a short one. Your composition will make better reading and will be neither boring nor overly complicated.

A paragraph is a series of sentences that develops a unified thought. The lead sentence presents the topic that is to follow. Then, subsequent sentences detail in logical order its substance. The last sentence in a paragraph should conclude the topic.

Sentences within a paragraph should build one upon another. A completed composition will have continuity and style if each sentence, and then each paragraph, is smoothly joined to the next.

E. APPRAISING AND OUTLINING EACH ASSIGNMENT

You don't have to plan to fail; all you have to do is fail to plan.

Anonymous

Written assignments indicate your grasp of class work. Obviously, it is important that you know exactly what is expected of you in each instance. The most common assignments are either reports or research papers. Appraise what you are being asked to write. Think about the research, reading, and writing you will have to do. And be sure to allow yourself plenty of time to meet the deadline

Reports are a test of your ability to understand and react to something you have read. An instructor usually expects a short sum mary of the content of the book or article, your comments on the author's presentation and style, your personal reaction to the work, and an evaluation of its importance.

Research papers are a test of your ability to choose a topic, investigate it, organize the material, and then write about it clearly and accurately. When you are asked to choose a topic, be realistic about your choice. Can you handle it? Does your library have enough resource books? Four or five sources, at least, should be used. The most effective way to collect data is to use index cards. Each card should indicate the source, author, publisher, date, and page number. After you have completed the research, arrange the cards in a sequence that will allow you to write about the subject with continuity and coherence .

Before you begin writing a report or paper, it is always best to make an outline of what you plan to say. Outlines are as indispensable to such writing as blueprints or drawings are to carpenters. First, write down the main headings, leaving several lines of space in between. Then, under each of the headings, list the subheadings that are to be covered. Identify the specific points that should be developed under the subheadings, and so on. When the blueprint of the material is complete, you are ready to start writing. Organize your outline well, follow it carefully, and your written presentation will reflect a logical and thorough development of the subject.

F. WRITING, REVIEWING AND REVISING

Those who write dearly have readers, those who write obscurely have commentators.
Albert Camus

When you are ready to start writing, make sure that you have your reference notes and books nearby, a good light, and good writing tools. Plan to work without interruption for one or two hours. Your outline will serve as your guide.

Even the most accomplished writers expect to make many revisions. So, when you write the first draft, concentrate on content and clarity more than on style. It is a good idea to leave plenty of space between lines for the corrections, additions, and polishing that will come later.

The introductory paragraph in a composition should give a clear idea of what you are setting out to do. Subsequent paragraphs should develop the main idea in an orderly way, with each paragraph containing a transition from the preceding one. The final paragraph should summarize and conclude what has been said. By reading the first and last paragraphs of most non-fiction writing, you should be able to grasp both premise and conclusion of an author's thoughts.

After you have completed the initial draft, put it aside for two or three days. Come back to review it when you are fresh. Be a stern critic. Have you started each heading or subheading with a topic sentence or paragraph that states what you are setting out to do? Do the main sections and subdivisions present the material clearly? Have you omitted points that you listed in the outline? Is there unnecessary or repetitious information? Does the conclusion summarize what has gone before? Are your footnotes and bibliography correct?

Once you have gone over the draft for content and accuracy, review and edit it for style. Try to read as objectively as you can. Remember the underlying importance of grammar and criticize your use of words, phrases, clauses, sentences, and paragraphs. Does one thought flow evenly and obviously from another?

You might want to change the sequence of sentences or paragraphs for better presentation. If so, cut, shift, and staple new parts together. Try to be as brief as possible. Delete what is superfluous and distracting to your main thoughts. It has been said that crisp writing usually has a good deal of shortening in it! The total effect must be readable. Rewrite a section if necessary. Remember that carelessness in spelling, punctuation, and capitalization will also influence the quality of your work.

Now you are ready to make the final copy. Type it if you can, or write very legibly with a carbon copy for future reference. Leave generous margins on the left and right sides of each page. When you have finished, proofread the paper, making any corrections neatly. Review your references or footnotes once again for accuracy. It is always a good idea to prepare a title page and, if possible, to submit the completed assignment in a folder or binder

Your grades may depend on how well you have mastered these writing techniques. When your marked paper has been returned, review the instructor's comments-you can learn from mistakes you might have made. Remember that how well you write will also be an important measure of your success after you leave school. With patience and hard work, you can experience the satisfaction of being happy with the content and style of your work. The choice of words is right, the grammar is correct, the flow of language is smooth, and it says just what you hoped it would! That is the reward of a successful writer.

G. GLOSSARY

1. *Grammatical Terms*

GRAMMAR The study of language and the proper use of words and word construction.

RHETORIC Refers to the correct choice and use of words in a way that gives style to written or spoken prose.

COMPOSITION The process of putting together or writing a complete work of prose, usually non-fiction.

SYNTAX That part of grammar which deals with sentence structure.

SUBJECT The word(s) in a sentence about which something is asserted or asked.
The students in the classroom read the science textbook.

PREDICATE The word(s) that asserts something about the subject of a sentence and, therefore, consists of a verb and its modifiers.
The students in the classroom read the science textbook.

MODIFIER A general term for the word(s) that qualifies or describes other words in a sentence. It is usually an adjective or an adverb, or an adjectival or adverbial phrase.
The students in the classroom read the science textbook.

OBJECT The word(s) describing the person or thing that directly or indirectly completes the action of the verb.
The students in the classroom read the science textbook.

CLAUSE A group of words which contains both a subject and a predicate but does not constitute a complete sentence.
The *aged woman*, although she appeared to be in good health, was gravely ill.

PHRASE A group of related words without a subject or a predicate.
The aged woman, although appearing to be *in good health*, was gravely ill.

PARTICIPLE A verbal adjective, usually derived from the present or past participle of a verb.
The *aged woman, although appearing to be in good health, was gravely ill.*

GERUND A verb form that ends in-ing and acts as a noun.
The aged woman, although *appearing* to be in good health, was-gravely ill.

INFINITIVE A verb form preceded by the word to. It can serve as a noun, adjective, or adverb.
The aged woman, although appearing to be in good health, was ill (used as verb).
The aged woman was too ill to fight (as adverb).
To write well takes practice (as noun).

ACTIVE VOICE Refers to a verb whose subject is performing the action. Paul caught the Frisbee.

PASSIVE VOICE Refers to a verb whose subject is acted upon.
The Frisbee was caught by Paul.

PREFIX The beginning of a word. It is attached to the root, or word base, to make a new word.
Refuse, to use again; or, undertake, to take on.

SUFFIX The ending of a word. It is added to the root, or base word, to make a new word.
Admirable worthy of praise; or, walker, one who walks.

2. *Major Classifications of Sentences*

I. According to Structure:

SIMPLE SENTENCE Contains a single independent thought but may vary in length depending upon the number of modifying words, phrases, or dependent clauses it contains. *It has one subject and one predicate.*

COMPOUND SENTENCE Contains two or more independent clauses joined by a conjunction. *This sentence is compound, and its two clauses are linked by the conjunction and rather than being separated by a period.*

COMPLEX SENTENCE Contains one independent clause and one or more dependent clauses. *While this clause is dependent, this second clause is Independent.*

II. According to Expression:

DECLARATIVE SENTENCE Makes a statement.
This is a declarative sentence.

IMPERATIVE SENTENCE Voices a command.
Start your homework as soon as you can.

INTERROGATIVE SENTENCE Asks a question.
Do you agree with this example?

EXCLAMATORY SENTENCE Utters a cry or emotion.
How lucky we all are!

3. *Parts of Speech*

NOUN Identifies the persons or things or ideas in a sentence.
Jim and his *friend* jogged around the *campus*.

PRONOUN Used in place of a noun.
Jim and *his* friend jogged around *their* neighborhood.

VERB Expresses the existence or action of the subject in the sentence.
Jim jogged every afternoon.

ADJECTIVE Qualifies or describes (or modifies, as grammarians say) nouns or pronouns.
Jim and his athletic friend jogged around the large reservoir.

ADVERB Modifies, or qualifies, verbs, adjectives, or other adverbs and is most often formed by addingly to an adjective.
Jim and his friend jogged *happily* every morning.

CONJUNCTION Joins two or more words, phrases, or clauses together within a sentence. Common conjunctions include: and, but, not, or, yet, after, because, since, where, and so forth.
Jim and Paul jogged and then rested because they were tired.

PREPOSITION Indicates a relationship between a noun or pronoun and some other word(s) in a sentence. Common prepositions include: *of*, *on*, *to*, *at*, *by*, *for*, *from*, *in with*, *above*, *against*, *like*, *toward*, and so forth.
Jim and Paul went for a swim in the pool.

INTERJECTION An independent word(s) that expresses an exclamation or emotion. It has no grammatical function in a sentence. Ouch, ah, oh, hey are examples. *Ouch, my foot hurts!*

4. *Punctuation Marks*

PERIOD Marks the end of a complete idea.

COMMA Indicates a short pause between separate, related words or ideas.

SEMICOLON Indicates a longer pause than a comma; it takes the place of a conjunction between independent clauses.

COLON Indicates that a number of things is to follow.
The plane's itinerary was: New York, Philadelphia, Baltimore, and Richmond.

QUESTION MARK Used at the conclusion of a complete question.

DASH Used to show a break of emphasis in thought.
Properly used–not overly used–dashes can be very effective.

EXCLAMATION POINT Manifests strong emotion. What a pity the child was crippled!

HYPHEN Connecting link between two parts of a word, either because it is brokeh at the end of a line, or because it is a combination of two parts, such as *self-evident* or *heavy-handed*.

APOSTROPHE Indicates either the possessive form of nouns and indefinite pronouns or the omission of a letter. The word *it's* is a contraction of *it is*, not the possessive form that you would use if you were talking about your *pencil's eraser or shirt's button*.

QUOTATION MARK Enclose exact words, titles, or passages. Single marks are used to show a quotation within a quotation. Mary's first sentence quoted Lincoln: "My favorite speech in history begins, 'Fourscore and seven years ago.'"

PARENTHESES Set off material that is supplementary (not necessary) to the main thought.

IV. HOW TO PREPARE FOR A WRITTEN EXAMINATION

A. COMMENTARY

The key to both success and enjoyment in an examination lies in your ability to use time wisely. You need to establish a pattern of good study habits and skills. Such habits and skills will help you get the necessary work done as the months and years go by, and you will handle exams with a minimum of stress and a maximum of achievement.

Authorities in education generally agree that successful preparation for an examination starts in the beginning of each course and continues throughout. Four overall steps are suggested:

1. Make a course study plan
2. Use good review techniques
3. Pace the exam carefully
4. Reassess your grades and work

B. MAKING A STUDY PLAN

1. *At the beginning of each course, develop a daily schedule* that allows time for preparation, study, review, recreation, eating, and sleeping. Your ability to adhere to the plan will be a measure of your success.

2. *A study area, conducive to learning, is important.* Make sure it has good light and all the tools you will need. Before the term starts, have on hand the texts, study guides, outlines, dictionaries, and reference books, paper, pads, notebooks, and pens that will allow you to concentrate without interruption.

3. *Study and review differ from each other.* As they are equally important, allocate time for both in your daily schedule. Study refers to learning new material for the first time. Review is critical because it strengthens the retention of this new knowledge.

4. *Forgetting takes place most rapidly immediately after learning.* Review and recall, therefore, is more effective soon after study. Following each session, go over the main points for 10 to 15 minutes to reinforce them in your memory. This makes reviewing for exams later a quicker, simpler task.

5. *Don't overtax your memory or stamina.* Research shows that most people can absorb and retain just so much knowledge at one time. It's important to learn day by day, week by week. But each period of study scheduled into your work plan should be no longer than 1 or 11/2 hours, followed by recreation, meal, or other activity.

6. *Take legible course and study notes.* Mark the margins and underline your textbooks throughout the course, and you will be able to review for weekly quizzes or final exams with a minimum of strain.

C. USING EFFECTIVE REVIEW TECHNIQUES

If you have applied yourself during the course, then preparing for exams is largely a question of review. The time needed is not so extensive as some students think-provided you have been working consistently. Review for weekly quizzes should take no more than 15 minutes, a mid-term hour exam 2 or 3 hours, and a final examination 5 to 8 hours.

1. *Your preparation for a final should be carefully scheduled* into the two weeks prior to exam day. Organize a schedule that does not interfere with your regular study for on-going courses. Beware of racing your motor. Make sure you still allow time for rest and relaxation, with no longer than 1 or 1½ hours of review at one time. Your mind needs breaks.

2. *Plan your review systematically and consistently.* Go from main idea to main idea, using the textbook chapter headings or your instructor's term outline as a guide. Go from chapter notes to chapter notes or from class notes to class notes, recalling the important headings and ideas in each. If certain points are difficult for you to remember, then reread the textbook. Otherwise, stick with your notes. Don't plan to learn something for the first time.

3. *Making summary notes is often helpful*, depending on the amount of material to be reviewed. In 4 to 8 pages, you can outline the main points of your detailed class and text chapter notes. Headings with indented numbered points under them make relationships more obvious. This procedure will also help reinforce the major ideas and important details.

4. *Summary notes can also serve as a self-test* toward the end of your preparation for exams. Put a sheet over each page and slowly uncover the first heading-see if you remember the main points under it. As you go, ask yourself what, when, etc.

Try to predict the exam questions. Be alert throughout the term to the emphasis instructors put on certain topics, aspects, or ideas. They often give clues to points that are important or particularly need review.

5. Ask your instructor what he recommends for pre-examination work. Use his comments as a guide but don't try to outguess him.

6. *Group reviewing can he helpful.* But it shouldn't take the place of working on your own. Limit discussions of significant points and possible test questions to 30 or 45 minutes, with no more than 4 or 5 people.

7. *Avoid cramming.* If you have followed a regular schedule of study and review, you should not have to cram the last day. Remember, forgetting takes place more rapidly right after learning. If you do have to cram, be selective. Don't attempt an exhaustive review.

D. USING SPECIAL EXAMINATION SKILLS

1. When the exam begins, listen to the instructions and then start reading through the entire test. Organize your thoughts.
2. *Budget time for each question.*
3. *Think carefully about one question at a time.*
4. *Jot down key words as guides for your writing.*
5. *Write legibly.*
6. *Short-form or objective questions demonstrate your ability to recognize details* and your judgment in choosing among alternatives. Attention must be given to key words like: all, none, never, might, or should. Avoid leaving blanks, an answer might be correct even though you are not sure.

7. Essay *questions test your ability to express yourself*, to interpret and to organize material.
8. *Finish each question as well as you can.*
9. *Make answers as concise and clear as possible.*
10. *Reread everything carefully* after you have answered all the questions

E. LEARNING FROM YOUR WRITTEN WORK

When you receive your grades and get back exam booklets, read over the answers. Compare them to your textbook and class notes in order to check mistakes and find out why or how you answered incorrectly. If you don't understand your instructor's marks, ask him where you went wrong. This re-evaluation will help you recognize faults in your study skills. Learn by your mistakes and go on to the next phase of enjoyable and successful course work.

ANSWER SHEET

ST NO. ______________ PART ______ TITLE OF POSITION ______________________________

(AS GIVEN IN EXAMINATION ANNOUNCEMENT - INCLUDE OPTION, IF ANY)

ACE OF EXAMINATION ______________________________ DATE ______________

(CITY OR TOWN) (STATE)

RATING

USE THE SPECIAL PENCIL. MAKE GLOSSY BLACK MARKS.

1 A B C D E	26 A B C D E	51 A B C D E	76 A B C D E	101 A B C D E
2 A B C D E	27 A B C D E	52 A B C D E	77 A B C D E	102 A B C D E
3 A B C D E	28 A B C D E	53 A B C D E	78 A B C D E	103 A B C D E
4 A B C D E	29 A B C D E	54 A B C D E	79 A B C D E	104 A B C D E
5 A B C D E	30 A B C D E	55 A B C D E	80 A B C D E	105 A B C D E
6 A B C D E	31 A B C D E	56 A B C D E	81 A B C D E	106 A B C D E
7 A B C D E	32 A B C D E	57 A B C D E	82 A B C D E	107 A B C D E
8 A B C D E	33 A B C D E	58 A B C D E	83 A B C D E	108 A B C D E
9 A B C D E	34 A B C D E	59 A B C D E	84 A B C D E	109 A B C D E
10 A B C D E	35 A B C D E	60 A B C D E	85 A B C D E	110 A B C D E

Make only ONE mark for each answer. Additional and stray marks may be counted as mistakes. In making corrections, erase errors COMPLETELY.

11 A B C D E	36 A B C D E	61 A B C D E	86 A B C D E	111 A B C D E
12 A B C D E	37 A B C D E	62 A B C D E	87 A B C D E	112 A B C D E
13 A B C D E	38 A B C D E	63 A B C D E	88 A B C D E	113 A B C D E
14 A B C D E	39 A B C D E	64 A B C D E	89 A B C D E	114 A B C D E
15 A B C D E	40 A B C D E	65 A B C D E	90 A B C D E	115 A B C D E
16 A B C D E	41 A B C D E	66 A B C D E	91 A B C D E	116 A B C D E
17 A B C D E	42 A B C D E	67 A B C D E	92 A B C D E	117 A B C D E
18 A B C D E	43 A B C D E	68 A B C D E	93 A B C D E	118 A B C D E
19 A B C D E	44 A B C D E	69 A B C D E	94 A B C D E	119 A B C D E
20 A B C D E	45 A B C D E	70 A B C D E	95 A B C D E	120 A B C D E
21 A B C D E	46 A B C D E	71 A B C D E	96 A B C D E	121 A B C D E
22 A B C D E	47 A B C D E	72 A B C D E	97 A B C D E	122 A B C D E
23 A B C D E	48 A B C D E	73 A B C D E	98 A B C D E	123 A B C D E
24 A B C D E	49 A B C D E	74 A B C D E	99 A B C D E	124 A B C D E
25 A B C D E	50 A B C D E	75 A B C D E	100 A B C D E	125 A B C D E

ANSWER SHEET

TEST NO. ______________ PART ______ TITLE OF POSITION ______________________________
(AS GIVEN IN EXAMINATION ANNOUNCEMENT - INCLUDE OPTION, IF ANY)

PLACE OF EXAMINATION ______________ (CITY OR TOWN) ______________ (STATE) DATE ______________

RATING

USE THE SPECIAL PENCIL. MAKE GLOSSY BLACK MARKS.

1 A B C D E	26 A B C D E	51 A B C D E	76 A B C D E	101 A B C D E
2 A B C D E	27 A B C D E	52 A B C D E	77 A B C D E	102 A B C D E
3 A B C D E	28 A B C D E	53 A B C D E	78 A B C D E	103 A B C D E
4 A B C D E	29 A B C D E	54 A B C D E	79 A B C D E	104 A B C D E
5 A B C D E	30 A B C D E	55 A B C D E	80 A B C D E	105 A B C D E
6 A B C D E	31 A B C D E	56 A B C D E	81 A B C D E	106 A B C D E
7 A B C D E	32 A B C D E	57 A B C D E	82 A B C D E	107 A B C D E
8 A B C D E	33 A B C D E	58 A B C D E	83 A B C D E	108 A B C D E
9 A B C D E	34 A B C D E	59 A B C D E	84 A B C D E	109 A B C D E
10 A B C D E	35 A B C D E	60 A B C D E	85 A B C D E	110 A B C D E

Make only ONE mark for each answer. Additional and stray marks may be counted as mistakes. In making corrections, erase errors COMPLETELY.

11 A B C D E	36 A B C D E	61 A B C D E	86 A B C D E	111 A B C D E
12 A B C D E	37 A B C D E	62 A B C D E	87 A B C D E	112 A B C D E
13 A B C D E	38 A B C D E	63 A B C D E	88 A B C D E	113 A B C D E
14 A B C D E	39 A B C D E	64 A B C D E	89 A B C D E	114 A B C D E
15 A B C D E	40 A B C D E	65 A B C D E	90 A B C D E	115 A B C D E
16 A B C D E	41 A B C D E	66 A B C D E	91 A B C D E	116 A B C D E
17 A B C D E	42 A B C D E	67 A B C D E	92 A B C D E	117 A B C D E
18 A B C D E	43 A B C D E	68 A B C D E	93 A B C D E	118 A B C D E
19 A B C D E	44 A B C D E	69 A B C D E	94 A B C D E	119 A B C D E
20 A B C D E	45 A B C D E	70 A B C D E	95 A B C D E	120 A B C D E
21 A B C D E	46 A B C D E	71 A B C D E	96 A B C D E	121 A B C D E
22 A B C D E	47 A B C D E	72 A B C D E	97 A B C D E	122 A B C D E
23 A B C D E	48 A B C D E	73 A B C D E	98 A B C D E	123 A B C D E
24 A B C D E	49 A B C D E	74 A B C D E	99 A B C D E	124 A B C D E
25 A B C D E	50 A B C D E	75 A B C D E	100 A B C D E	125 A B C D E